Chris Wright and James Cousins mince no words in this straightforward work, identifying the problem with the shortfall in funding for ministries as *our* problem. This is an unequivocal call to the body of Christ to take personal ownership of the unmet needs of the ministries we support and to respond through generous and joyful giving. They call on us to become both sowers and kingdom builders, two powerful metaphors they reinforce through the stories of Moses, David and Paul. With this new teaching added to John Stott's *The Grace of Giving* and Chris Wright's *The Gift of Accountability,* we have a powerful presentation of kingdom values applied to the practice of asking and giving. I pray that God's people will take the challenge of *The Shortfall* to heart, resulting in a new wave of generosity for God's work.

R. Scott Rodin, PhD
Senior Consultant and Chief Strategy Officer, The Focus Group
Author, *The Sower, The Third Conversion,* and *The Steward Leader*

I was challenged by the title of this book as I have not only faced this issue of shortfall personally with missions I have founded and chaired but also as chairman and trustee of several donor foundations and trusts and the overwhelming and continual requests for funds to help with ministry shortfalls. Chris Wright and James Cousins have done a great service to the Christian community in producing a practical resource that not only draws extensively from biblical principles but also includes the powerful testimony of a businessman and how he began to think through and address this issue of the shortfall in practical ways over a period of several years. It does not need to take us several years! The very clear and hard-hitting message in their book put simply is: "The shortfall is not their problem but my problem."

Ram Gidoomal, CBE
Chairman, South Asian Concern
Former Chairman, Stewardship Services UK
Former Chairman, The Lausanne Movement International Board

Please read this book. Read it with an open heart; it will challenge you. Read it with an open mind; it will impact how you view your life and how you could live it by God's grace. Every disciple of Christ needs to hear and embrace this rich biblical teaching. I would even encourage you to pray the Lord's prayer before and after each time you sit down with this wonderful book. Ask the Lord how he would have you not only pray toward the hallowing of his name and the coming of his kingdom but also be a part of the answer to your own prayer, so that God's will for his people and the world will be done.

Michael Oh, PhD
Global Executive Director/CEO,
Lausanne Movement

In this new preface to John Stott's *The Grace of Giving*, Chris Wright and James Cousins identify the core problem with a lack of funds for Christian ministries and then ask the tough question: Who is responsible for the shortfall? While the challenge is confronted head-on with a call for all of us to "provide" for the work of those who are called to be in "ministry," I appreciate the fact that the authors also charge those who are seeking funds to properly communicate their needs to those who have the means to share God's resources with them.

Brad Layland, CFRE
CEO, The FOCUS Group

Needs in the world have never been greater and opportunities for our witness to the gospel of Jesus Christ in word and deed more plentiful Moreover, never have Christians had more resources. If we are gripped by the kingdom of God, this should challenge us to seize the day with greater generosity and stewardship. But selfishness, confusion, and limited vision cripple our mission. This book, combining the wisdom of James Cousins, Chris Wright and John Stott, offers wise advice on needs, giving and accountability necessary for God's mission. I pray that many will rise up to the challenge of this book, and that it will lead to a greater commitment to partner with God in his mission with our financial resources.

Michael W. Goheen, PhD

Director of Theological Education, Missional Training Center

Professor of Missional Theology,

Covenant Theological Seminary, Creve Coeur, Missouri, USA

The Shortfall

*Owning the Challenge of
Ministry Funding*

Christopher J. H. Wright
with James Cousins

Includes
The Grace of Giving
by John Stott

Part 1 and Part 3 text © 2021 Christopher J. H. Wright

Part 2 revised text © 2021 The Literary Executors of John R. W. Stott. Published with permission.

Part 2 original text © 2008 John R. W. Stott. Originally published by the Lausanne Movement under the title *The Grace of Giving: Ten Principles of Christian Giving*.

Epilogue @ 2021 James Cousins

Published 2021 by Langham Global Library
An imprint of Langham Publishing
www.langhampublishing.org

Langham Publishing and its imprints are a ministry of Langham Partnership

Langham Partnership
PO Box 296, Carlisle, Cumbria, CA3 9WZ, UK
www.langham.org

ISBNs:
978-1-83973-095-5 Print
978-1-83973-096-2 ePub
978-1-83973-097-9 Mobi
978-1-83973-098-6 PDF

British Library Cataloguing-in-Publication Data
A catalogue record for this book is available from the British Library.

ISBN: 978-1-83973-095-5

Cover & Book Design: projectluz.com

Contents

Preface

This little book has a rather varied history. Part 2 originated as an exposition by John Stott of 2 Corinthians 8–9 entitled, "Ten Principles of Christian Giving." It was first delivered at The Gathering in San Diego in 1998, then preached at All Souls Church, Langham Place, London, and published successively by Generous Giving, the International Fellowship of Evangelical Students (IFES), and Didasko Files. It continued to be a very popular little booklet for many years. It is reprinted here as part of this book by permission of the Literary Executors of John R. W. Stott.

Part 3 originated as an exposition by Chris Wright of the same chapters, focusing not so much on the principles of Christian giving as on the accountability of those who handle the fruit of it – the actual money given. This exposition was first given at a conference of the Korean Global Mission Leaders Forum on the topic of "Accountability in Mission," held at the Overseas Ministries Studies Center in New Haven, Connecticut, USA, in 2013. It was first published by Didasko Files in 2013.

The combination of the two expositions by John Stott and Chris Wright was later published in 2016 by Hendrickson Publishers for the Lausanne Library, entitled *The Grace of Giving: Money and the Gospel*, and later still in 2019 as *Money and the Gospel: Giving Money with Grace, Handling Money with Integrity*, by Dictum Press. We gratefully acknowledge Julia Cameron's kind co-operation in enabling these two expositions to be incorporated into this new book.

Part 1, however, is a completely fresh and hitherto unpublished reflection. It arose from a conversation between Chris Wright and James Cousins, a Christian businessman in Northern Ireland. James shared with Chris his enthusiasm for "the little green book" as he called the Stott-Wright booklet described above, and he had given it widely to friends and colleagues in the business and professional world.

"However," he said, "There's a problem with it. It talks about the *solution*: how Christians should be giving money, and how they should be handling money. But it doesn't talk about the *problem*." James was referring to the problem of the shortfall in funding that so many Christian ministries and mission agencies face. And the real problem, James went on to explain, is not just who faces that shortfall, but who *owns* it. That is, who does God hold responsible to address that shortfall and do something about it? The shortfall, James insisted, should not be seen just as a problem for the ministries, but as a problem to be owned by those to whom God has entrusted the means to supply what is needed to solve it. Including himself.

"*We* need to own the problem!" James concluded.

Over some further conversations and email exchanges, with diagrams and charts, James explained his thinking further, accompanied by his friend Harry Robinson, executive director of One Another Ministries. Meanwhile Chris found that James's perspectives resonated in his own mind with several strands of biblical texts and examples. Such a biblical foundation would sit very appropriately with the expositions of 1 and 2 Corinthians in "the little green book." So the idea emerged that Chris should write an additional section based on James's thinking to stand alongside, and provide an essential context for, the earlier work of John Stott and himself. And that is how part 1, and indeed the concept for this new book, came into existence.

Together James, Harry, and Chris pray that God will use this small offering to challenge and change some well-worn patterns of thought and practice in the whole area of Christian giving. And we'd like to think that John Stott would have given his approval to this further lease of life for one of the many gems in his vast literary legacy.

Chris Wright and James Cousins
May 2020

Part 1

The Problem of the Shortfall

Chris Wright with James Cousins

Introduction

Why is it that so much Christian mission and ministry seems to lack adequate funding? Why does it seem that those who have wonderful visions and plans for the work God has given them to do in serving the kingdom of God and engaging in all kinds of gospel-centred activities so often find that their income falls short of their budgets, let alone their visions?

Later in this book, we will see just how clearly the Bible teaches that Christian giving always should be a response to God's grace to us in the gospel. It is because we have *received* so much from God in Christ – so immeasurably much – that we should be motivated to respond with generous giving to the Lord and his work. But if Christian giving is a response to the gospel, why is it (to repeat) that so much gospel ministry seems to lack adequate funding? Why is there so often a *shortfall* between the vision that God gives to agencies of Christian mission and the resources to fulfil that vision? And whose problem is that shortfall? These are the questions we address in part 1.

1. Funding Christian Mission

There are many forms of ministry and mission. That is to say there are multiple ways in which Christians can serve God by serving others, multiple ways in which they participate in God's mission of bringing healing and reconciliation to his whole creation through Christ (Eph 1:9–10). Ministry and mission, in general terms, embrace the whole of life, including our homes and families, our vocation and work in the so-called secular world, all our relationships and engagement in society, under the Lordship of Christ. In that fully biblical sense, ministry is far wider than the work of those we ordain as "ministers," and mission is far wider than the calling of those we send as "missionaries." All disciples of the Lord Jesus are called into all kinds of ministry and mission in every area of life in the world – and *some* are called into particular forms of ministry and mission that need to be financially supported by other believers within the fellowship of the church. It is this latter group that we are thinking of in this section. But it is important to recognize that *all of us*, whether paid by the church or not, are committed to ministry and mission in the name of Christ at the very heart of our identity and role as Christians in God's world.

Financial support for Christian mission agencies comes in a number of different patterns, partly depending on the nature of the agency. Let's survey some of the ways that Christian mission is funded.

Some agencies facilitate the sending of large numbers of *people* into cross-cultural mission – whether for direct evangelism and church planting or a wide range of other work that embodies the gospel and is done in the name of Christ, such as in medicine and health; education; poverty and debt relief; community development; engineering; creation care; advocacy and action for the enslaved, trafficked, or imprisoned; conflict resolution and reconciliation; and many more. Other agencies require less personnel but are heavily invested in *projects and initiatives* that require funding, such as publication of Christian literature, infrastructure needs in health and education, clean water, and so on.

In the first category, sending *people*, many agencies expect their mission partners to "raise their own support." But that is a broad term that can be fulfilled in a number of ways, each of which can claim some biblical authority.

Some people are prepared to follow in a fairly rigorous way the instructions Jesus gave to his disciples when he first sent them out on their missionary journeys – that is, not to take money with them but to be dependent on those they would live among (Matt 10:9–13). The Alliance for Vulnerable Mission[1] has adopted this approach by depending entirely on locally available resources and local languages as a way of overcoming the perception (and sadly often the reality) of missionaries being those who impose a damagingly Western mindset and money-based power and influence on traditional cultures and communities.

Some "raise their own support" by following Paul's example and earning money through carrying on their own trade or profession in another country. From Paul's example, this is known as "tent making" (Acts 18:1–3; 1 Cor 9:10–18; 2 Thess 3:6–9), and large numbers of Christians in cross-cultural contexts follow this model. They engage in honest entrepreneurial business, often giving employment, or they

---

1. "Alliance for Vulnerable Mission," *Vulnerable Mission* (6 March 2018), http://www.vulnerablemission.org/.

offer their professional training and skills, for example in teaching, or law, or agriculture, or engineering, and earn their living in the place to which they believe God has called them. They then live and bear witness to Christ and share the life of the local church if there is one, supporting themselves (and sometimes others) by their own earnings.[2]

Some follow not so much Paul's *example* as Paul's *principle* (to which he made himself an exception!), that churches have a responsibility to provide adequately for the needs of those who serve them or work for the gospel (1 Cor 9). So they lay their needs before Christian friends and churches and either explicitly ask for financial support with appropriate budgeting, or where their agencies or their own principles disallow that, pray that God will motivate others to give the required amounts.

In this category of mission life and service, often the larger share of personal support will typically come from a wide group of known and faithful individual friends who regularly give modest amounts and pray for their missionary friends. A further share will come from a few supporting churches with mission budgets who commit to sending and supporting these partners in mission. Likewise, mission agencies that support many individuals tend to have income streams that reflect these proportions: the highest percentage coming from individual donors, some from churches, and occasionally some larger gifts or legacies.

On the other hand, agencies in the second category that initiate and manage larger *projects* may typically require larger capital gifts to provide the kind of sustained and multi-

---

2. The Lausanne Movement has several networks committed to tentmaking mission. See "Tentmaking," https://www.lausanne.org/networks/issues/tentmaking; "Business as Mission," https://www.lausanne.org/networks/issues/business-as-mission; and "Workplace Ministry," https://www.lausanne.org/networks/issues/workplace-ministry.

year income that such projects may need. In this case, the balance of the income stream may look different. They will of course seek the support of individuals and churches who share their vision and objectives, but they will also hope and work for very substantial gifts from foundations and trusts as well as individual Christians to whom God has entrusted significant wealth. It is probable that Lydia – a house-owning business woman in a high-end textile market and probably independently wealthy – was instrumental in initiating the financial gift that the church in her city of Philippi sent to Paul for his missionary work further south (Acts 16:13–15, 40; Phil 1:3–5; 4:10–19).

Now none of these approaches or patterns should be seen as "the right one," or "more biblical" than another. As we have seen, each of them can cite biblical precedents. Equally, all of them have their own strengths and weaknesses, and wise agencies will weigh these up and seek the best balance of methods for their own funding needs.

And of course we cannot even suggest that the person who can give only small amounts to the Lord, but does so faithfully and often, is any less important to God or to God's work than the donor who comes forward with six- or seven-figure donations. We know that God certainly does not think that way. "God loves a cheerful giver," said Paul (2 Cor 9:7), no matter what the size of the cheerful gift! Jesus completely contradicts any idea that big donors matter more than small ones. In fact, big donors may be giving relatively *a lot less* of their actual wealth than smaller donors. That's what Jesus observed about the widow who gave all she had to live on, her two small coins, contrasted with the rich people who gave but a fraction of what they could have given (Luke 21:1–4). In the estimation of Jesus, the widow's small offering was actually a *larger* gift than the impressive donations by the wealthy.

It is also very obvious that there will always be far more of the former than the latter. That is, there are far more people who can and do give small amounts regularly than there are super-wealthy people who are able to make mega gifts. We cannot put hard percentages on the breakdown of the sources of overall global Christian giving. It must vary greatly from country to country and ministry to ministry. Wise agencies, of course, will have done some research on the spread and pattern of their particular donor base.

But we might, purely as a guess, imagine that for every thousand regular donors of smaller amounts, there could be perhaps ten who could be major donors. And one can scale upwards on a similar ratio. These fewer donors are those to whom God has entrusted such wealth that they can, in some cases, single-handedly fund a large portion of the whole vision of an agency. And in many cases, it will be that approximately 1 percent who provide, or would be capable of providing, some 60 percent of a ministry's income. That's worth repeating.

Approximately 1 percent of donors provide, or are capable of providing, some 60 percent of a ministry's income. It looks like the chart on the opposite page. We will explain what we mean by "kingdom builders" a little bit later.

2. Working Together for the Truth

From the breadth of the Bible's teaching, we can see that God intends that God's people should be generous and systematic in providing for those whose whole lives are dedicated to the service of God, people who do not have other sources of income from land or employment.

The prime example of this principle in the Old Testament is the tribe of the Levites. They were not assigned any land in the division of the territory among the tribes after they settled in Canaan under Joshua – though they were given towns

KINGDOM BUILDERS

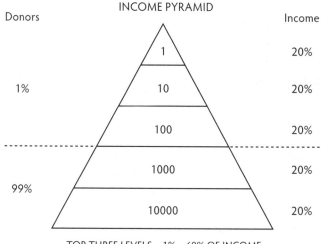

INCOME PYRAMID

Donors

Income

1	20%
10	20%
100	20%
1000	20%
10000	20%

1%

99%

TOP THREE LEVELS = 1% = 60% OF INCOME
BOTTOM TWO LEVELS = 99% = 40% OF INCOME

"And the Lord said to Paul . . . Do not be afraid . . .
For I am with you . . . For I have many in this city who are
my people." Acts 18:9–10

Kingdom builders believe
God has his people in every city of the world

with some pasture lands (Josh 21). Rather, the Lord himself was their "portion," since they served God, initially in the tabernacle and eventually in the temple (Deut 18:1–5). Since they had no income from tribal land, they were completely dependent on the tithes and offerings of the rest of the people. They were not to be forgotten when the nation celebrated its festivals (Deut 14:27; 16:11, 14). And God saw very clearly when the people were failing in that responsibility (Mal 3:8–10). This instruction to Old Testament Israel that they must materially support the Levites stands as a scriptural precedent that Paul himself cites as one of his arguments concerning the duty of Christian churches to provide for the needs of those who preach the gospel (1 Cor 9:13–14).

As for the New Testament, most of us are probably fairly familiar with Paul's teaching in 1 and 2 Corinthians, and we will come back to that teaching in parts 2 and 3. But another much overlooked, small corner of the New Testament makes a very similar point – namely 3 John. The elder John is writing to Gaius, presumably the pastor of a church with which John has connections. John commends Gaius for his faithfulness. Gaius has been faithful not only to the truth of the gospel (vv. 3–4), but also in what he and his church have been doing for the brothers and sisters who were coming to his church as part of an itinerant ministry (vv. 5–8).

We know that in the early church, there were these men and women who travelled from region to region, sometimes as evangelists like Paul and his team, sometimes as teachers who strengthened the young churches, like Apollos (Acts 18:27–28). They were first-century itinerant missionaries in many ways, crossing land and sea to spread the gospel and serve the churches. Now in what John says about these sisters and brothers, and the response of Gaius's church to them, we can see three things. There is *sending* (3 John 6), *going* (v. 7), and *supporting* (v. 8).

When John asks Gaius to "*send them on their way* in a manner that honours God" (3 John 6), he doesn't just mean, "wave them good bye and sing a nice hymn as they board the ship." No, the Greek word was a technical term for making all of the advance preparations for someone going on a journey, including providing food and money, arranging transport if possible, paying fares, providing letters of identity and commendation, etc. And the reason John gives these instructions is that these people were travelling "for the sake of the Name" (meaning Jesus) and were "receiving no help from the pagans" – that is they had no other "secular" means of support (v. 7). If they were *going*, then somebody was *sending*. Finally says John it is our duty to "show hospitality to such people" (v. 8), which again means more than a nice cup of tea and a bed for the night. It speaks of substantial provision for their needs, what we would call financial *support* and other gifts in kind.

So this little letter of 3 John is a fascinating insight into early church missionary support and how it spoke of faithfulness – faithfulness to the truth matched by faithfulness to God's servants. The second half of the letter shows an ugly contrast, but we needn't go there now.

As a final thought, look how John finishes his commendation of Gaius. "We ought therefore to show hospitality to such people *so that we may work together for the truth*" (3 John 8).

Work together! It's not that the itinerant missionaries are out there working for the truth and the church members back home just give them financial help so they can get on and do that job. They do the work; we pay the bills. No, *we are all in this together*, says John. Christian giving to Christian ministry is an integral and essential part of working for the truth – the truth of the whole biblical gospel that the world so desperately needs to hear and to see in action.

Christian giving is itself a spiritual ministry; so therefore is the task of motivating, enabling, and administering it. Raising and providing the funds by which ministry can be supported is an essential spiritual part of gospel ministry for the sake of the kingdom of God, as Paul and John saw and taught very clearly. Let's never refer to those who actively seek and motivate Christian giving as "*just* fundraisers"! We are all "working together for the truth."

Because we are all doing this together, we also have to insist that the modest giver of regular small amounts among the bottom ten thousand of our giving pyramid is "working together for the truth" just as much as the mega donor who is in the top 1 percent. Both of them are working alongside the evangelist, preacher, teacher, or Christian missionary of a hundred varieties. All of us – whether sending, going, or supporting – are "working together for the truth."

So the Bible gives some great teaching and examples. But we still have to come back to our issue: the financial shortfall so many ministries face.

3. The Shortfall: Whose Problem Is It?

> Depend on it. God's work done in God's way will never lack God's supply. He is too wise a God to frustrate His purposes for lack of funds, and He can just as easily supply them ahead of time as afterwards, and He much prefers doing so.

So said the famous James Hudson Taylor, founder of the mission agency originally to China and now known as OMF. It's a much-quoted saying. We all probably know inspiring stories of people who have been blessed with miraculous provision of their financial needs at just the right time to enable them to serve God in this way or that. And we might point to Bible verses that support such confidence.

And yet, and yet . . . For every miracle story like that, we probably know far more situations, friends, mission agencies, and ministries of all sorts that seem painfully short of the money needed to fulfil their vision. If that situation goes on a long time, it can be crippling to a ministry and spiritually so discouraging for all involved. "They need more faith!" we exclaim. "Or more prayer." Yet for all their faith and prayer, it seems the shortfall stays stubbornly stuck. Why is that? What's the problem? Why the shortfall?

We need to be ruthlessly honest at this point and read Hudson Taylor's words carefully. He does specify that it must be "God's work," and that it should be "done in God's way." So if a ministry is always short of money, it *could* be that one or other of these prerequisites is missing, or even both. Not all apparently Christian ministry is "God's work." Jesus warned us very soberly indeed about that (Matt 7:21–23). And even if a ministry has no shortfall, and, on the contrary, even if it is raking in lots of prosperity, that may be something diametrically other than "God's supply." Not all Christian mission is being "done in God's way" if there are issues of un-Christlike power structures, lack of transparency and integrity, unethical practices, and so on. We cannot expect God to give his abundant supply if God's own standards and principles of Christian behaviour are being flouted.

So, if I am a potential Christian donor (small or large), and I encounter a ministry that is in constant shortfall for lack of funds, I will be wise to exercise some discernment, ask some serious questions, do my homework. Is this genuinely God's work being done in God's way, for which I might play some part in God's supply? If I find no such assurance, then I should look elsewhere.

But even when we exclude rogue ministries or agencies that we instinctively avoid, we shall surely encounter many Christian ministries and mission agencies who we can most confidently affirm *are* doing God's work in God's way, and yet still experience the constant challenge of a shortfall in the funding they need to do all that they believe God is calling and envisioning them to do. Vision always seems to outstrip their income. The annual budget is a constant struggle to decide what can be funded and what must be cut back or dropped altogether. Staff or ministry partners may live on the edge of uncertainty as to whether their salaries or allowances will be paid. Carefully planned projects may have to be postponed or pared back. Glaring needs that they are eager to meet may remain glaringly unmet. Exciting opportunities that ignite imagination and prayer may fall depressingly to the ground for want of funds to take them up. Strategic plans bathed in prayer and hard thinking may end up only partially fulfilled and partially frustrated.

And that in essence is the problem of the shortfall. Whatever Hudson Taylor said, it seems that in many places and for many of God's faithful servants, God's work being done in God's way *is* lacking the fullness of God's supply.

So the question is this: Where does the problem lie? Whose problem is it? Who needs to own the problem of the shortfall?

Now presumably we can immediately agree that the problem does not lie with God. For as Hudson Taylor added, "God is not willingly going to frustrate his own purposes for lack of funds." The question is, Where are those funds? And where are they not?

We immediately think of *where those funds are not* – namely with the Christian ministries who need them. It's their problem! They have a shortfall because they lack funds, and that's a problem. Their problem. That's why they have to keep working so hard to make up the shortfall with ever more imaginative forms of fundraising and donor development and so on. The funding shortfall is their big problem. God bless them, we pray, and please help them solve their funding problem.

But here's the thing. Here's the challenge that we really want to get across as emphatically as we can. This is the crucial point. This is what this section of our book is all about.

What if we stop thinking that the problem lies only with where the funds are lacking? What if the problem really lies with *where the funds already are?*

If God's work done in God's way should never lack God's supply, then wherever there is a lack (the shortfall), *there is a problem at the supply end.* And if that is not *God's* fault, then it must be that the problem lies with those who have the means and power to be the *agents* of God's supply. The supply lines have got blocked. There is a breakdown between God's supply and those entrusted to deliver it. That's the problem. This is where the problem lies.

We believe that in this whole matter of Christian giving – the subject of this whole book – we need to address the problem of the shortfall by acknowledging where the problem really lies. Of course the shortfall *is* a problem for ministries and mission agencies that lack the funds to accomplish all God has given them to do. But the problem is not theirs alone, or even mainly. Fundamentally the problem lies with those to whom God has entrusted the means to accomplish his purposes, those to whom God gives the responsibility of delivering God's supply for God's work done in God's way. The problem lies at the supply end – but not with God.

Or to put it more bluntly, if I am a person to whom God has given some capacity for giving to God's work – and that must mean all of us, however much or little, but especially those with a large capacity – then when I become aware of a godly ministry that is short of funds for God's work, I should not be thinking, "That's a real problem for them." No, it's a problem for *me*.

The shortfall is not "their problem." The shortfall is my problem.

It is my problem because I am one of those whom God holds responsible for channelling resources that God has entrusted to me, which come from God and belong to him anyway, into the work that God wants to be done. And as long as people like me fail in that responsibility and so create a shortfall in the funding of God's work, then *the problem is ours before God.* Or putting it another, we are a problem to God, since we are hindering the accomplishment of his purposes.

Now don't misunderstand us. There is an important caution here of course. We are not saying that every time we individually see or hear about some need, some shortfall in Christian funding, we are obligated immediately to give money to meet that need. In that way lie all kinds of guilt, manipulation, and exhaustion. For the needs are vast, and the more we know about them, the more stressed we could feel. No, we are not saying that every Christian has to be giving to every needy Christian ministry or mission. Accepting that we collectively own *the* problem does not mean we have to solve *every* problem ourselves.

No, we are simply getting at the basic principle that the problem of the shortfall should not rest solely on the shoulders of *those who suffer it*, but should be owned and addressed by *those with the capacity to do something about it*. And that of course needs all the proper thoughtful and prayerful consideration we can give to discern priorities and make personal decisions, choosing both the direction of our individual giving and working together in local churches to do the same. God does not expect everybody to give to everything. But he does expect every Christian to be intentionally and prayerfully giving to *some* thing. As Jesus himself put it, "From everyone who has been given much, much will be demanded; and from the one who has been entrusted with much, much more will be asked" (Luke 12:48).

So the question becomes this: Do we have the courage and commitment to go to our sisters and brothers who are striving to do God's work in wide and varied Christian ministries but who are facing shortfalls in their funding and to encourage them (and challenge ourselves) with this perspective? Are we willing to say to them,

> Please tell us clearly about your vision and plans. Tell us what you believe God is calling you to do. And also tell us honestly about your financial needs. *You may think that the shortfall is your*

problem. But it is not. It is ours. Under God *we* will own the problem, and with God's help, *we* will address it.

4. The Bible Addresses the Problem

This may feel like a new and somewhat upside-down way of thinking about the issue. But there is plenty of biblical support for putting it this way round. In any case, we need to make sure that the Bible is our authority and inspiration, not just Hudson Taylor!

The Old Testament has a lot to say about issues of financial need in different contexts. What is interesting is that Israel's law never addresses the ones who are poor and in need, telling *them* what to do to solve their problem. Rather all the laws about economic issues (including about necessary lending and borrowing, indentured labour, payment of vulnerable workers, redemption of land or debt slaves, etc.), are addressed to *those who held economic power*: the lender, the landowner, the employer, etc.

For example, the lender is commanded to act compassionately towards the borrower, "and it will be regarded as a righteous act in the sight of the LORD your God" (Deut 24:6, 10–13). Conversely, the employer who fails to pay a poor and needy worker proper wages in a timely manner (daily), "will be guilty of sin" (Deut 24:14–15). There's a problem! Not just a problem for the poor worker, but a problem for the well-endowed employer who fails in his duty and thereby commits sin before God. The law makes it clear that *God* sees that a worker who lacks money has a problem. Of course he does. Any of us could see that too today. But from God's point of view, the problem is not with the worker but with the one who is not stewarding the wealth God has enabled him to create (Deut 8:17–18) to deal justly with his workforce. And that employer could be a woman as much as man, as the responsibility and integrity of the "Wife of Noble Character" show (Prov 31:14–20).

James echoes this law in Deuteronomy, sounding like one of the prophets, and shows how serious that "problem" will be for such people – *they* are the problem in God's view.

> Now listen, you rich people, weep and wail because of the misery that is coming on you. Your wealth has rotted, and moths have eaten your clothes. Your gold and silver are corroded. Their corrosion will testify against you and eat your flesh like fire. You have hoarded wealth in the last days. Look! The wages you failed to pay the workers who mowed your fields are crying out against you. The cries of the harvesters have reached the ears of the LORD Almighty. You have lived on earth in luxury and self-indulgence. You have fattened yourselves in the day of slaughter. (Jas 5:1–5)

Job, who had been phenomenally wealthy before the calamities struck him (Job 1:1–3), knew he would have had a serious problem before God if he had failed to give generously to the needy. *Their* shortfall was *his* problem when he had the power to do something about it.

> If I have denied the desires of the poor
>   or let the eyes of the widow grow weary,
> if I have kept my bread to myself,
>   not sharing it with the fatherless –
> but from my youth I reared them as a father would,
>   and from my birth I guided the widow –

> if I have seen anyone perishing for lack of
>   clothing,
>   or the needy without garments,
> and their hearts did not bless me
>   for warming them with the fleece from my
>   sheep,
> if I have raised my hand against the fatherless,
>   knowing that I had influence in court,
> then let my arm fall from the shoulder,
>   let it be broken off at the joint.
> *For I dreaded destruction from God,*
>   *and for fear of his splendor I could not do such*
>   *things.* (Job 31:16–23; my emphasis)

The New Testament puts the emphasis in the same way. We've already referred to James. Here he is again. Very pointedly, James puts the problem of the shortfall – the needs of a poor brother or sister – into the lap of the one who has the ability to help but fails to.

> Suppose a brother or a sister is without clothes
> and daily food. If one of you says to them, "Go in
> peace; keep warm and well fed," but does nothing
> about their physical needs, what good is it? In the
> same way, faith by itself, if it is not accompanied
> by action, is dead. (Jas 2:15–17)

John makes a very similar point, significantly linking practical love to the example of God in Christ, which will be our major focus in part 2.

> This is how we know what love is: Jesus Christ laid
> down his life for us. And we ought to lay down
> our lives for our brothers and sisters. If anyone
> has material possessions and sees a brother or
> sister in need but has no pity on them, how can

> the love of God be in that person? Dear children,
> let us not love with words or speech but with
> actions and in truth. (1 John 3:16–18)

Finally, let's look at an interesting example of this principle at work in the book of Acts when the problem of a shortfall is owned by those who had the ability to address it. When a coming famine threatened the believers in Judea with impending poverty and hunger, what did God do? He did not send a prophet to Jerusalem to warn them they had a problem coming, telling them that they needed to prepare for it and do some urgent fundraising in advance. No, God sent a prophet, Agabus, *to Antioch* to make the believers there aware of the danger threatening their sisters and brothers in Judea. So as soon as they were alerted by the Holy Spirit to a threat facing their fellow believers, it became *their* problem, and they set out to solve it by collecting funds that could be sent to meet the shortfall in Judea. *Judea's* anticipated shortfall was accepted as *Antioch's* problem, for they had the ability to help.

> During this time some prophets came down
> from Jerusalem to Antioch. One of them,
> named Agabus, stood up and through the Spirit
> predicted that a severe famine would spread over
> the entire Roman world. (This happened during
> the reign of Claudius.) The disciples, as each one
> was able, decided to provide help for the brothers
> and sisters living in Judea. This they did, sending
> their gift to the elders by Barnabas and Saul. (Acts
> 11:27–30)

So Paul's first missionary journey with Barnabas, sent by the church in Antioch under the guidance of the Holy Spirit, was not their evangelistic trip to Cyprus and Asia Minor in Acts 13, but this one for *famine relief* in Acts 11, a mission which they completed and returned to Antioch (Acts 12:25).

This first experience of being sent by the church under the instruction of the Holy Spirit seems to have made a permanent impression on Paul and shaped his mission theology and practice. For not only did he eagerly "continue to remember the poor" (Gal 2:10), but he put a great deal of time and effort into encouraging and enabling the Gentile churches in Greece to make a financial gift to alleviate the poverty of the Jewish believers in Jerusalem. That, of course, is the background to the biblical texts that we shall study in greater depth in parts 2 and 3.

But again from the point of view of our argument here, notice how Paul describes his fundraising efforts when writing to the Christians in Rome. He sees this gift as the Gentile believers somehow *discharging a debt*. They *owe* it to make this gift. It was a responsibility they had taken on, a problem they had the power to address, indeed a privilege they begged to be part of.

> Now, however, I am on my way to Jerusalem in the service of the Lord's people there. For Macedonia and Achaia were pleased to make a contribution for the poor among the Lord's people in Jerusalem. They were pleased to do it, and indeed they owe it to them. For if the Gentiles have shared in the Jews' spiritual blessings, they owe it to the Jews to share with them their material blessings. (Rom 15:25–27; see also 2 Cor 8:3–4)

So then we think there is good biblical support for saying that wherever there is serious need among God's people – when there is a shortfall, in other words – *the problem of the shortfall belongs to those who have the power to address it, not just to those who suffer it.*

It's not just their problem; it's our problem!

Now we can immediately agree that this principle applies whether you think of yourself as among the 99 percent who may not be able to give much but can certainly give something ("every one according to his ability," says Luke about the giving of the Christians in Antioch; Acts 11:29, ESV) or among that 1 percent entrusted by God with very significant wealth that could make a game-changing difference to some of the ministries doing God's work in God's way. All we can say, in line with the principle that Jesus himself laid down, is that the more you have the power to give, the greater is your responsibility.

Or more bluntly, in a Christian world of shortfalls and needs, the more God has given you, the more you own the problem. To repeat,

> From everyone who has been given much, much
> will be demanded; and from the one who has
> been entrusted with much, much more will be
> asked. (Luke 12:48)

5. Sowers and Kingdom Builders

But how do we know when there is a shortfall, or where the most serious and damaging shortfalls in the funding of God's work are happening? This calls for good, clear, honest, and understandable communication from ministries and mission agencies. And that information then needs to be shared with others in a way that informs and inspires, so that God's people can shoulder the problem and address it generously and adequately.

"Ask God and Tell His People." This is a financial policy that originated with one well-known mission agency and is now shared by several.

Now the first part is so simple but also the most important part, of course: "Ask God" through prayer that the Lord will bless the ministry through the provision of resources that the ministry needs. But the second part, "Tell His People," is where it can easily go wrong.

Notice that it says "*Tell* His People"; it does not say "*Ask* His People." We need to *tell* people what the ministry is trying to do in the name of Jesus. We must communicate the story, and only then ask people to partner with us in this kingdom ministry. Some ministry people make the mistake of asking for money instead of building up a relationship by communicating well with God's people and praying that God would touch their hearts through his Holy Spirit to support the ministry.

We could use the imagery of sowers and builders here. Both are biblical images.

Sowers

Sowers are those who sow the seed of good information about particular ministries, people who have a passionate commitment to that ministry by way of their own prayer and giving and who intentionally share their passion with a number of others as opportunity arises. They may not themselves be anywhere close to being "major donors," though they may be, of course. But they have one prime asset: enthusiasm for the cause and personal investment in it. As they invest their own enthusiasm in others, they sow the seed for a multiplication of giving – some of which might turn out to be very substantial.

Potential sowers can readily be found among that 99 percent of modest but regular givers. Could you be one of them? Perhaps you already are. Here are some ways in which ordinary Christian supporters of ministries and mission agencies can be effective sowers in ways that really bear fruit:

- Become a representative for the society or ministry in your local church, encouraging the church to include them in their mission giving budget and sharing news and needs from the ministry.
- Host small events in your own home when the work can be presented to friends using the agency's resources – literature, videos, etc. – or inviting a speaker to share their work and vision.
- Volunteer with the organization in various capacities so as to increase your personal involvement and understanding of their work and their needs.
- Highlight the ministry on your social media outlets by posting or forwarding publicity information, stories, news of events, etc.
- Collaborate with a group of friends to contribute regularly to a mission partner's financial budget and to pray for them while doing so.

Why not ask God if there are ways you could be a sower for his kingdom by being an enthusiastic advocate and communicator for a Christian ministry that fires your own imagination, faith, and commitment?

Kingdom Builders

All of us who are disciples of the Lord Jesus Christ are commanded by him to seek first the kingdom of God and his righteousness (Matt 6:33). So all of us, whatever level of income or wealth God entrusts to us, are to be engaged in the task of building his kingdom. Now of course, that language can be a bit misleading. The kingdom of God belongs to God, and it is God who builds it! "The kingdom of God" is a way of speaking of the sovereignty of God in creation, in providence, in redemption, and in grace. Nevertheless, the amazing truth is that God calls us to participate with him in his sovereign plans and purposes for his whole world. We are, as Paul described himself and his fellow workers, "God's fellow workers" (1 Cor 3:9, ESV) – an amazing job description.

You may have heard of the mouse and the elephant crossing a bridge. When they got to the other side, the mouse turns to the elephant and says, "Boy, did we make that bridge shake!" Rather more elephant than mouse! Likewise, the kingdom is God's, the mission is God's, the work is God's, the glory is God's, and the bridge shaking is God's! And yet, and yet . . . he invites us to *work with him in partnership.* To build together with him in the cause and goals of his kingdom. What a privilege!

And here's the thing. That privilege of being a kingdom builder belongs to every believer. There are no elite vs ordinary Christians, no aristocracy and peasantry, no "great and good" and the "hoi polloi," no "major and minor donors." We are *all* equally members of one body, branches in Christ's vine, sheep in God's flock, living stones being built into God's temple, citizens of God's kingdom, children of one Father, followers of one Lord, sharers in one Spirit, sisters and brothers in one family, and the household of God.

This wonderful truth of the spiritual equality of all believers in Christ needs to be stated as emphatically as we can before we go any further. We want every reader of this book, of whatever economic status, to know yourself to be a kingdom builder, called to contribute and share in the privilege and blessing of participating with God in his great mission for all creation and all human history by giving generously in response to God's grace. For every one of us, this is a privilege and joy. And for every one of us also, this is an inescapable responsibility. Every one of us is part of God's "supply chain" to ensure that God's work done in God's way will not lack God's supply.

For most of us, who come somewhere within the broad spectrum of that 99 percent, being a kingdom builder means regular giving in modest amounts according to our income and ability. That is where God calls us to be faithful, generous, sacrificial, and committed. That is God's call on every believer. Is it a call and commitment that you accept: that to be a disciple of Christ is to be a kingdom builder for God through your committed giving?

But then within that great army of kingdom builders – the whole church – there are what we might call "the 1 percent kingdom builders." They are those kingdom builders to whom God has entrusted a larger portion of wealth than the average Christian believer. This might be inherited wealth from parents or grandparents. Or it might be wealth built up over several decades through successful entrepreneurship in business. Or it might have come through the hard work involved in studying and training for some highly paid profession, and then successfully exercising it and reaping the rewards.

Whatever the source, you know that in all honesty, you belong within that top 1 percent of the Christian giving community. And you know too that you are there only by God's grace and blessing, by the gifts and abilities God has given you, by the opportunities of education and advantageous family and friends, and by the health and strength and daily breath that have proved God's unfailing love. Yes of course, it is likely you worked very hard and long to get where you are, and nobody begrudges the rewards this work has brought. But in your reflection as a child of God, you fully take to heart the admonition of Deuteronomy 8:17–18, and do so with gratitude.

> You may say to yourself, "My power and the
> strength of my hands have produced this wealth
> for me." But remember the LORD your God, for it
> is he who gives you the ability to produce wealth.

The challenge then is also to take to heart those unambiguous words of Jesus that from those to whom much has been entrusted, much will be required (Luke 12:48).

Those who *can* give the most *should* give the most.

That's Jesus talking.

So the question we have to lay before you is this: Are you going to use the wealth God has entrusted to you to build for the kingdom of God with larger building blocks than most Christians can afford? Most people can offer a few bricks. And, sure, millions of small bricks rightly used can build spectacular edifices. But in comparison to the average small brick, you can afford to offer blocks like the ones that built the pyramids. What are you using them to build, and for whom? For the kingdom of self, or the kingdom of God?

Or to put it more directly, will you ask God what part of the shortfall in the funding of some Christian ministry does God want you personally to own and address? Will you change your thinking and praying from seeing that shortfall as "*their* problem" to shouldering it as "*my* problem"? Will you then take practical steps to find out how you can address that problem you are now willing to share? Where will you, as a kingdom builder for God, invest the resources he has entrusted to you, and do so *in a major and significant way*?

In the Epilogue you can read the personal testimony of a businessman who discovered how he needed to answer exactly those questions, James Cousins, whose thinking helped to inspire and shape this part 1.

6. Two Biblical Kingdom Builders

But isn't it wrong to talk about money and get involved in all this fundraising business? Or embarrassing at least! For some people, this topic is quite a stumbling block. At one level, many of us are simply culturally disinclined to talk about money at all – especially our own – still less to ask for money, even for a good cause like the work of God's mission. But at a more serious level, there are some mission societies and individuals who hold a conscientious conviction or principle that we ought not to ask for money because we should not need to. God knows our needs and the needs of whatever ministry or task he himself has called us into, so we should trust God to provide. "Ask God," they'd agree, but then trust God, without asking his people. It is a principle adopted by several "faith missions" – they live and work by faith and prayer and trust God to supply their needs since the work and the funds alike belong to God.

These are convictions that we certainly respect in those who hold and live by them. However not all would agree, and there are some signal events in the Bible where some quite overt "fundraising" was done, when people were explicitly *asked* to give generously *and did so*. In parts 2 and 3, we shall explore the apostle Paul's fundraising efforts in which he quite clearly asked the Gentile churches in Greece to contribute funds towards the gift he wished to make on their behalf to the Jewish believers in Jerusalem. But we can see at least two Old Testament examples as well.

Moses

On Mount Sinai, God gave Moses instructions for the plan and construction of the tabernacle that he wanted the people of Israel to build for him. These are recorded in detail in Exodus 25–31. But then came the terrible rebellion of the golden calf, when the people came very close to being destroyed altogether. Only by God's grace were they restored and the story could move on (Exod 32–34). After that restoration, the time came for the construction of the tabernacle to begin. Moses rises magnificently to the occasion with a very detailed "ask" in Exodus 35. He knew what is needed, and he spells it out to the people. He knew God's plan, and he told God's people. Here is an inspired fundraiser at work!

> Moses said to the whole Israelite community, "This is what the LORD has commanded: From what you have, take an offering for the LORD. Everyone who is willing is to bring to the LORD an offering of gold, silver and bronze; blue, purple and scarlet yarn and fine linen; goat hair; ram skins dyed red and another type of durable leather; acacia wood; olive oil for the light; spices for the anointing oil and for the fragrant incense; and onyx stones and other gems to be mounted on the ephod and breastpiece.
>
> "All who are skilled among you are to come and make everything the LORD has commanded. . . ."
>
> Then the whole Israelite community withdrew from Moses' presence, and everyone who was willing and whose heart moved them came and brought an offering to the LORD for the work on the tent of meeting, for all its service, and for the sacred garments. All who were willing, men and women alike, came and brought gold jewelry of all kinds: brooches, earrings, rings and ornaments. . . .
>
> All the Israelite men and women who were willing brought to the LORD freewill offerings for all the

work the LORD through Moses had commanded
them to do. (Exod 35:4–10, 20–22, 29)

Notice several things about this wonderful moment.

- First, it was in response to God's command (at the beginning and end of our quotations), but God's *command* had followed immediately from God's forgiving *grace*. This is the same pattern that we shall see in Paul's writing: all our giving is a matter of obedience responding to grace.

- Second, Moses is quite explicit and detailed in telling the people exactly what was needed. He did not leave them to guess, or just "be led by the Lord." He simply told them specifically what was needed and asked for it.

- Third, their gifts were to be "from what you have" – people were to give as they were able.

- Fourth, there is a repeated emphasis on the word "willing" – this was voluntary, even though it was an obedient response to a command. This giving was an act of the heart. It may sound paradoxical, but this outpouring of giving was *commanded* but not *compulsory*. Even in the time of Moses, it seems, God loved a cheerful giver!

- Fifth, the gifts were not just material possessions like gold and silver, precious stones and fine cloths, etc. Some gave their skills and time as craftsmen to do the work. Indeed, Bezalel and Oholiab, the leaders of the skilled people, are the first people in the Bible who are described as filled with God's Spirit (Exod 31:1–11; 35:30–36:1).

- Finally, the whole community was involved, expressly both men and women. Biblical generosity is gender inclusive, as Lydia would doubtless agree.

David

Moses's great festival of giving in the wilderness to build the tabernacle was matched by David's great festival of giving in Jerusalem to enable his son Solomon to build the temple. The account is in 1 Chronicles 29, and it resonates with some of the same warm notes that we heard above. It would be worth pausing to read 1 Chronicles 29:1–20 as a fitting climax to this first part of our book and as motivation to pray about how you will personally respond to what you've been reading. Why not get the Bible open and read 1 Chronicles 29:1–20 now?

As you read through that story, take note of these points.

- Like Moses, David is quite specific in listing all the necessary materials for the temple, then states what he personally has given, and then asks the people directly, "Now, who is willing to consecrate themselves to the LORD today?" (1 Chr 29:5). So David makes the plan very clear, specifies what is needed, and then invites God's people to join with him in generous giving.
- Remarkably, the leaders took the lead. David's generosity as king was immediately followed by substantial giving by the various ranks of leadership among the people (vv. 6–8), presumably because they had the most wealth to give. And I love the observation that, "The people rejoiced at the willing response of their leaders, for they had given freely and wholeheartedly to the LORD" (v. 9). It was not, as would likely be the case in so many churches and ministries today, that "the *leaders* rejoiced at the willing response of the *people*"! No, the leaders led by example and *their* presumably large gifts inspired the giving of the rest of the ordinary people. There's

an example for 1 percent kingdom builders to follow.

- Once again, we see the emphasis on how all this giving was "willingly" and "from the heart" (vv. 5–6, 9, 16–17). From Moses to David to Paul – they all happily affirm that "God loves a cheerful giver" (2 Cor 9:7).

- For David, this giving was a matter of praise and doxology. His hymn of thanksgiving centres on the cosmic reign of God, the God who rules all and gives all (1 Chr 29:10–13). David knew he was doing God's work in God's way and could trust in God's supply. But he also knew that God's supply would come through the generous giving of himself, his leaders, and the people.

- But then David spots just what a surprising paradox this moment truly is. We are only giving to God what already belongs to him, he says, in the sharp realization of verse 14. It was as if a tenant in a fully furnished home (which is what Israel was in Yahweh's land, v. 15; see Lev 25:23) were to take an item of furniture from the house and give it to the landlord as a birthday gift. What sort of gift is that? Everything in the house belongs to him already! Perhaps David has in the back of his mind that warning and truth that we read above: "You may say to yourself, 'My power and the strength of my hands have produced this wealth for me.' But remember the LORD your God, for *it is he who gives you the ability to produce wealth*" (Deut 8:17–18). That reminder applies to kingdom builders just as much as to kings.

- David sees that what God is really looking for is not the size of the gift but the integrity of the heart. So we finish with a verse that John Stott was very fond of quoting, "I know, my God, that you test the heart and are pleased with integrity. All these things I have given willingly and with honest intent" (1 Chr 29:17).

That should be the motto of every kingdom builder.

As we come to the end of part 1, let's return to the apostle Paul as we prepare to spend a lot time in his company in parts 2 and 3. And let's remember our main purpose in these pages. We've tried to encourage a radical shift in thinking about "the problem of the shortfall." We need to see it not just as a problem that has to be faced by ministries and missions that are striving to do God's work in God's way, but as a problem that needs to be *owned* by those to whom God has entrusted the task of providing God's supply. And that means all of us, as Paul would agree.

But Paul also had a word for the 1 percent kingdom builders of his own day – Christians who were among the wealthy few, probably very few at that time. Most believers came from the 99 percent of society (1 Cor 1:26). Paul has no hesitation in urging Timothy to make sure that those who have been blessed with this world's wealth understand their obligation to be generous.

> *Command* those who are rich in this present world not to be arrogant nor to put their hope in wealth, which is so uncertain, but to put their hope in God, who richly provides us with everything for our enjoyment. *Command* them to do good, to be rich in good deeds, and to be generous and willing to share. In this way they

will lay up treasure for themselves as a firm foundation for the coming age, so that they may take hold of the life that is truly life. (1 Tim 6:17–19; my emphasis)

For Paul, this was not a matter of warm-hearted, voluntary charity, but of straightforward obedience to God's command and investment in God's kingdom.

Well, it's not among the Ten Commandments. But it is still a biblical command, isn't it? The question is this: Is it a command that you are personally committed to obey?

Part 2

The Grace of Giving

John Stott

Introduction

When we become Christians, our giving has a new impetus. We are called to give generously, and with joy, as a fruit of the Spirit's life within us. The following pages take us through the apostle Paul's teaching on Christian giving, and draw out principles which we can apply to our own situation. I trust you will find it a helpful and provocative study, as I have found it to be myself.

In 2 Corinthians 8 and 9, Paul is explaining arrangements for an offering from the Greek churches of Achaia and Macedonia for the impoverished churches of Judea. We also read about it in Romans 15 and 1 Corinthians 16. Paul did not see giving as a mundane matter, nor as something on the periphery of church life. On the contrary, he saw the grace of giving as a core part of what it means for us to be members of Christ's church.

He shows how our regular giving is rooted in three central themes in the gospel: the grace of God, the cross of Christ, and the unity of the Spirit. It is very moving to grasp this combination of profound Trinitarian theology and practical common sense, as we shall see.

Here are Paul's ten principles. We start at the beginning of 2 Corinthians 8.

1. Christian Giving Is an Expression of the Grace of God

> And now, brothers, we want you to know about the grace that God has given the Macedonian churches. In the midst of a very severe trial, their overflowing joy and their extreme poverty welled up in rich generosity. For I testify that they gave as much as they were able, and even beyond their ability. Entirely on their own, they urgently pleaded with us for the privilege of sharing in this service to the Lord's people. And they exceeded our expectations: They gave themselves first to the Lord, and then by the will of God also to us. So we urged Titus, just as he had earlier made a beginning, to bring also to completion this act of grace on your part. (2 Cor 8:1–6)

Paul does not begin by referring to the generosity of the churches of Macedonia in northern Greece. He starts instead with "the grace that God has given to the Macedonian churches" (v. 1). Grace is another word for generosity. In other words, behind the generosity of Macedonia, Paul saw the generosity of God. Our gracious God is a generous God, and he is at work in his people to make them generous too.

Three tributaries come together in the river of Macedonian generosity, namely their severe trial, their overflowing joy, and their extreme poverty (v. 2). In consequence, the Macedonians gave even beyond their ability (v. 3), and they pleaded for the privilege of doing so (v. 4). How easily our comfortable

Western culture can deaden our sensitivity to others' needs. The Macedonians had no such comfort, and no such lure of personal satisfaction. Their values were entirely different. They gave themselves first to the Lord, and then to Paul and his fellow workers (v. 5). What a model for the Corinthians, and for us.

We read next how Paul had urged Titus to complete what he had begun in Corinth, the capital of Achaia, some time before (v. 6). What had Titus begun? He had been exhorting the Corinthians to give in the same way as the Macedonians.

This then is where Paul begins – with the grace of God in the Macedonian churches of northern Greece and with the same grace of God in the Achaian churches of southern Greece. Their Christian generosity is an outflow of the generosity of God.

2. Christian Giving Can Be a *Charisma*, That Is a Gift of the Spirit

> But since you excel in everything – in faith, in speech, in knowledge, in complete earnestness and in the love we have kindled in you – see that you also excel in this grace of giving. (2 Cor 8:7)

The Corinthians already excel in the spiritual gifts of faith, speech, knowledge, earnestness, and love, and the apostle urges them to excel also "in this grace of giving." Similarly in Romans 12:8 Paul includes among another list of charismata contributing to the needs of others. "… if it is to encourage, then give encouragement; if it is giving, then give generously; if it is to lead do it diligently; if it is to show mercy, do it cheerfully."

The grace of giving is a spiritual gift.

Many of God's gifts are generously bestowed in some measure on all believers and given in special measure to some. For example, all Christians are called to share the gospel with others, but some have the gift of an evangelist. All Christians are called to exercise pastoral care for others, but some are called to be pastors. Just so, all Christians are called to be generous, but some are given the particular "gift of giving." Those entrusted with significant financial resources have a special responsibility to be good stewards of those resources.

3. Christian Giving Is Inspired by the Cross of Christ

> I am not commanding you, but I want to test the sincerity of your love by comparing it with the earnestness of others. For you know the grace of our Lord Jesus Christ, that though he was rich, yet for your sake he became poor, so that you through his poverty might become rich. (2 Cor 8:8–9)

Paul was not commanding the Corinthians to give generously. This is not how he deals with them. Rather he puts the sincerity of their love to the test by comparing them with others and especially (it is implied) with Christ. For they knew "the grace of our Lord Jesus Christ."

Let us note this further reference to divine grace. The grace of God is at work in us (v. 1), and the grace of Christ challenges us to respond in like manner (v. 9). Let us not rush on, for here is one of the most searching principles Paul describes. Notice the two references to poverty and two references to wealth. Because of our poverty Christ renounced his riches, so that through his poverty we might become rich. It is not material poverty and wealth that Paul has in mind. No, the "poverty" of Christ is seen in his incarnation and especially his cross, while the "wealth" he gives us is salvation with all its rich blessings.

As we give, may we, too, reflect on the cross, and all that was achieved for us through the death of Christ. How meagre are our earthly riches in comparison.

4. Christian Giving Is Proportionate Giving

> And here is my judgment about what is best for you in this matter. Last year you were the first not only to give but also to have the desire to do so. Now finish the work, so that your eager willingness to do it may be matched by your completion of it, according to your means. For if the willingness is there, the gift is acceptable according to what one has, not according to what one does not have. (2 Cor 8:10–12)

During the previous year the Corinthian Christians had been the first not only in giving but in desiring to give (v. 10). So now Paul urges them to finish the task they had begun, so that their doing will keep pace with their desiring. This must be according to their means (v. 11). For Christian giving is proportionate giving. The eager willingness comes first; so long as that is there, the gift is acceptable in proportion to what the giver has (v. 12).

This expression "according to your means" might remind us of two similar expressions which occur in Acts. In Acts 11:29, members of the church in Antioch gave to the famine-stricken Judean Christians "as each one was able." In Acts 2 and 4, members of the church in Jerusalem gave "to anyone who had need" (Acts 2:45; 4:35).

Does this ring a bell in our memories? In his *Critique of the Gotha Programme* (1875), Karl Marx called for a society which could "inscribe on its banners 'from each according to his ability' and 'to each according to his need.'" I have often wondered if Marx knew these two verses in

Acts and if he deliberately borrowed them. Whatever our politics and economics may be, these are certainly biblical principles to which we should hold fast. Christian giving is proportionate giving.

Of course there are times when we are called to give as the Macedonians gave, out of proportion to their income, as a sacrificial offering in particular circumstances. But the principle here is a foundational one. Christian giving should never be less than proportionate to our income.

5. Christian Giving Contributes to Equality

> Our desire is not that others might be relieved while you are hard pressed, but that there might be equality. At the present time your plenty will supply what they need, so that in turn their plenty will supply what you need. The goal is equality, as it is written: "The one who gathered much did not have too much, and the one who gathered little did not have too little." (2 Cor 8:13–15)

Paul's desire, as he goes on to explain, is not that others may be relieved while they are hard pressed, for that would merely reverse the situation, solving one problem by creating another, but rather "that there might be equality" (v. 13). At present, Corinthian plenty will supply the needs of others, so that in turn, at a later stage, the plenty of others will supply Corinthian need. "The goal is equality" (v. 14). Paul illustrates the principle from the supply of manna in the desert. God provided enough for everybody. Larger families gathered a lot, but not too much. Smaller families gathered less, but not too little, and they had no lack (v. 15).

Paul is putting the affluence of some alongside the need of others, and calling for an adjustment, that is, an easing of need by affluence. This was with a view to *isotes*, the Greek word which can mean either "equality" or "justice."

What is this "equality" for which Paul calls? It has three aspects.

First, it is not egalitarianism. God's purpose is not that everybody receives an identical wage, lives in an identical house, equipped with identical furniture, wears identical clothing, and eats identical food – as if we had all been mass-produced in some celestial factory! No. Our doctrine of creation should protect us from any vision of colourless uniformity. For God the Creator has not cloned us. True, we are equal in worth and dignity, equally made in God's image. True, God gives rain and sunshine indiscriminately to both the evil and the good. But God has made us different, and has given his creation a colourful diversity in physique, appearance, temperament, personality, and capacities.

Second, it begins with equality of educational opportunity. Christians have always been in the forefront of those urging literacy and education for all. For to educate (*educare*) is literally to lead people out into their fullest created potential, so that they may become everything God intends them to be. For example, equal educational opportunity does not mean that every child is sent to university, but that every child capable of benefiting from a university education will be able to have one. No child should be disadvantaged. It is a question of justice.

Third, equality sees an end to extreme social disparity. Julius Nyerere, former president of Tanzania, said in his Arusha Declaration that he wanted to build a nation in which "no man is ashamed of his poverty in the light of another's affluence, and no man has to be ashamed of his affluence in the light of another's poverty."

The same dilemma confronts Western missionaries. Should they "go native," becoming in all things like the nationals they work among? Or should they continue to enjoy Western affluence without any modification of their lifestyle? Probably neither. The Willowbank Report on "Gospel and Culture" suggests that they should rather develop a standard of living "which finds it natural to exchange hospitality with others on a basis of reciprocity, without embarrassment."[1]

In other words, if we are embarrassed either to visit other people in their home, or to invite them into ours because of the disparity of our economic lifestyles, something is wrong; the inequality is too great, for it has broken the fellowship. There needs to be a measure of equalization in one or other direction, or in both. And Christian giving contributes to this equality.

6. Christian Giving Must Be Carefully Supervised

> Thanks be to God, who put into the heart of Titus the same concern I have for you. For Titus not only welcomed our appeal, but he is coming to you with much enthusiasm and on his own initiative. And we are sending along with him the brother who is praised by all the churches for his service to the gospel. What is more, he was chosen by the churches to accompany us as we carry the offering, which we administer in order to honour the Lord himself and to show our eagerness to help. We want to avoid any criticism of the way we administer this liberal gift. For we are taking pains to do what is right, not only in the eyes of the Lord but also in the eyes of man.

1. John Stott and Billy Graham, *Making Christ Known: Historic Mission Documents from the Lausanne Movement, 1974–1989* (Grand Rapids: Eerdmans, 1996), 82.

In addition, we are sending with them our brother who has often proved to us in many ways that he is zealous, and now even more so because of his great confidence in you. As for Titus, he is my partner and co-worker among you; as for our brothers, they are representatives of the churches and an honour to Christ. Therefore show these men the proof of your love and the reason for our pride in you, so that the churches can see it. (2 Cor 8:16–24)

Handling money is a risky business, and Paul is evidently aware of the dangers. He writes, "We want to avoid any criticism of the way we administer this liberal gift" (v. 20) and "we are taking pains to do what is right, not only in the eyes of the Lord but also in the eyes of man" (v. 21). He was determined not only to do right, but to be seen to do right.

So what steps did Paul take? *First*, he did not handle the financial arrangements himself, but put Titus in charge of them (vv. 16–17) and expressed his full confidence in him (v. 23). *Second*, Paul added that he was sending along with Titus another brother, who was "praised by all the churches for his service to the gospel" (v. 18). *Third*, this second brother had been "chosen by the churches to accompany" Paul and carry the gift (v. 19; see also 1 Cor 16:3). The people carrying the offering to Jerusalem had been elected by the churches because of their confidence in them.

It is wise for us now to take similar precautions against possible criticism. It is good for churches to be openly careful about the number of people present when the offering is counted, and for regular reports to be given to church members on the church finances. We need such transparency in church life; it gives confidence to the membership.

For mission agencies it is important to have a board giving wise and experienced oversight of the financial operations, so that money received from supporters can be invested well and pressed effectively into service. On a broader canvas, we can be thankful for the work of auditors, and for the government's oversight of all charitable giving through the Charity Commission, or its equivalent, which regulates both good practice and good reporting.

[We return to this issue in more detail in part 3.]

7. Christian Giving Can Be Stimulated by a Little Friendly Competition

> There is no need for me to write to you about this service to the Lord's people. For I know your eagerness to help, and I have been boasting about it to the Macedonians, telling them that since last year you in Achaia were ready to give; and your enthusiasm has stirred most of them to action. But I am sending the brothers in order that our boasting about you in this matter should not prove hollow, but that you may be ready, as I said you would be. For if any Macedonians come with me and find you unprepared, we – not to say anything about you – would be ashamed of having been so confident. So I thought it necessary to urge the brothers to visit you in advance and finish the arrangements for the generous gift you had promised. Then it will be ready as a generous gift, not as one grudgingly given. (2 Cor 9:1–5)

Paul had been boasting to the churches of northern Greece (e.g. Philippi) about the eagerness of the churches of southern Greece (e.g. Corinth) to give, and this enthusiasm had stirred the northerners to action (v. 2). Now Paul is sending the brothers already mentioned to Corinth to ensure that his boasting about the southerners will not prove hollow and that they will be ready as he had said they would be (v. 3).

For if some northerners were to come south with Paul and find the southerners unprepared, it would be a huge embarrassment. So Paul sent the brothers in advance, to finish the arrangements for their promised gift. Then they would be ready, and their gift would be generous and not grudging (v. 5). First Paul boasted of southern generosity, so that the northerners will give generously. Now he urges the southerners to give generously, so that the northerners will not be disappointed in them.

It is rather delightful to see how Paul plays off the north and the south against each other to stimulate the generosity of both. Competition is a dangerous game to play, especially if it involves publishing the names of donors and the amounts donated. But we can all be stimulated to greater generosity by hearing about the generosity of others.

In some churches the church council or elders are invited ahead of the rest of the congregation to pledge first to a church building project, and the total raised (without individual names) is announced before the church gift day. It can build faith for church members to know that their leaders are truly behind these special giving projects, where much sacrificial giving is needed.

8. Christian Giving Resembles a Harvest

Remember this: Whoever sows sparingly will also reap sparingly, and whoever sows generously will also reap generously. Each of you should give what you have decided in your heart to give, not reluctantly or under compulsion, for God loves a cheerful giver. And God is able to bless you abundantly, so that in all things at all times, having all that you need, you will abound in every good work. As it is written:

"They have freely scattered their gifts to the poor;
    their righteousness endures forever."

Now he who supplies seed to the sower and bread for food will also supply and increase your store of seed and will enlarge the harvest of your righteousness. You will be enriched in every way so that you can be generous on every occasion. (2 Cor 9:6–11)

Two harvest principles are applied here to Christian giving. *First*, we reap what we sow. Whoever sows sparingly reaps sparingly, and whoever sows generously reaps generously (v. 6). "Sowing" is an obvious picture of giving. What then can we expect to "reap"? We should not interpret Paul's point too literally, as if he were saying that the more we give, the more we will get. No. Each of us should give "what you have decided in your heart to give," neither reluctantly, nor under compulsion, but rather ungrudgingly, because "God loves a cheerful giver" (v. 7). Let's pause for a moment on that phrase "what you have decided in your heart to give." There is a sense here of a settled conviction about how much to give, of a decision reached after careful consideration, and always with joy and cheerfulness.

It is good to remind ourselves here of Paul's earlier letter to the Corinthians and his exhortation to systematic giving (1 Cor 16:1–3). Everyone should, he said, set aside a sum of money in relation to his income, "On the first day of every week" (v. 2). Our facility of setting up a bank transfer, for both our church giving and our mission giving, would be very much in keeping with this. We're reminded again here of the importance of "deciding." It is rarely necessary to give on the spur of the moment. How much better to take time and seek that settled conviction.

If we give in this spirit, what will happen? What harvest can we expect to reap? The answer is two-fold: (1) "God is able to bless you abundantly, so that in all things [not necessarily in material things] . . . having all that you need," and (2) "you will abound in every good work" because your opportunities for further service will increase (2 Cor 9:8). As the psalmist says, the consequence of giving to the poor is to have a righteousness which endures forever (v. 9; Ps 112:9).

Second, what we reap has a double purpose. It is both for eating and for further sowing. The God of the harvest is concerned not only to alleviate our present hunger, but to make provision for the future. So he supplies both "bread for food" (immediate consumption) and "seed to the sower" (to plant when the next season comes round). In the same way God will "supply and increase your store of seed and will enlarge the harvest of your righteousness" (2 Cor 9:10).

These verses are the origin of the concept of "seed money," expecting God to multiply a donor's gift. Paul is not teaching a "prosperity gospel," as some have claimed. True, he promises that "You will be enriched in every way," but he adds at once that this is "so that you can be generous on every occasion" (v. 11) and so increase your giving. Wealth is with a view to generosity.

9. Christian Giving Has Symbolic Significance

> Because of the service by which you have proved yourselves, others will praise God for the obedience that accompanies your confession of the gospel of Christ, and for your generosity in

> sharing with them and with everyone else. (2 Cor.
> 9:13)

There is more to Christian giving than meets the eye. Paul is quite clear about this. In the case of the Greek churches, their giving symbolized their "confession of the gospel of Christ" (v. 13). How is that?

Paul looks beyond the mere transfer of cash to what it represents. The significance was more than geographical (from Greece to Judea) or economical (from the rich to the poor). It is also theological (from Gentile Christians to Jewish Christians), for it was a deliberate, self-conscious symbol of Jewish-Gentile solidarity in the body of Christ.

Indeed, this truth, that Jews and Gentiles are admitted to the body of Christ on the same terms, so that in Christ they are heirs together, members together, and sharers together, was the "mystery" which had been revealed to Paul (e.g. Eph 3:1–9). This was the essence of his distinctive gospel. It was the truth he lived for, was imprisoned for, and died for. It is hinted at here, but elaborated in Romans 15:25–28.

Paul wrote there that the Gentile churches of Greece had been "pleased" to make a contribution for the impoverished Christians of Judea. "They were pleased to do it," he repeated. Indeed "they owe it to them. For if the Gentiles have shared in the Jews' spiritual blessings [culminating in the coming of the Messiah himself], they owe it to the Jews to share with them their material blessings" (Rom 15:27). It was a striking illustration and declaration of Christian fellowship.

In similar ways, our Christian giving can express our theology. For example, when we contribute to evangelistic enterprises, we are expressing our confidence that the gospel is God's power for salvation, and that everybody has a right to hear it. When we give to economic development, we express our belief that every man, woman, and child bears God's image and should not be obliged to live in dehumanizing circumstances. When we give to the maturing of the church, we acknowledge its centrality in God's purpose and his desire for its maturity.

10. Christian Giving Promotes Thanksgiving to God

> . . . and through us your generosity will result in thanksgiving to God.
>
> This service that you perform is not only supplying the needs of the Lord's people but is also overflowing in many expressions of thanks to God. Because of the service by which you have proved yourselves, others will praise God for the obedience that accompanies your confession of the gospel of Christ, and for your generosity in sharing with them and with everyone else. And in their prayers for you their hearts will go out to you, because of the surpassing grace God has given you. Thanks be to God for his indescribable gift! (2 Cor 9:11b–15)

Four times in the concluding paragraph of these two chapters, Paul states his confidence that the ultimate result of their offering will be to increase thanksgiving and praise to God. This is at the heart of all spiritual giving.

> Verse 11: "Your generosity will result in thanksgiving to God."
>
> Verse 12: "This service that you perform is . . . overflowing in many expressions of thanks to God."

Verse 13: "Others will praise God for the obedience that accompanies your confession of the gospel of Christ, and for your generosity."

Verse 15: "Thanks be to God for his indescribable gift!"

Authentic Christian giving leads people not only to thank us, the givers, but to thank God, and to see our gift to them in the light of his indescribable grace, shown supremely in the gift of his Son.

Conclusion

It is truly amazing that so much is involved in this transfer of money. We have the doctrine of the Trinity – the grace of God, the cross of Christ, and the unity of the Holy Spirit – and we have the practical wisdom of an apostle of Christ. Spiritual truth and practical wisdom both at work, side by side.

What an awesome privilege we have in helping others right across the world to give glory to God. Releasing more of the money which he has entrusted to us as stewards will end in this. And to increase thanksgiving to God for the sake of his own glory is surely our highest goal.

I hope that our study of these chapters will help to raise our giving to a higher level, and will persuade us to give more thoughtfully, more systematically, and more sacrificially. I for one (having preached this sermon to myself first) have already reviewed and raised my giving. I venture to hope that you may do likewise.

Part 3

The Gift of Accountability

Chris Wright

Introduction

To find out what the New Testament teaches about financial accountability in the church, and by extension in all Christian ministry and mission, let's look at the practice of the apostle Paul. As we saw in part 2, Paul had called for a collection of money from the churches in Greece (as we would now call it), that is, in the two Roman provinces of Macedonia in northern Greece and Achaia in southern Greece. He oversaw arrangements for this collection to be taken to the believers in Jerusalem, where there seems to have been a great deal of poverty among the believers. Paul clearly thought that it was very important for one part of the Christian church to help another in this way.

Paul's references to this collection of money for the poor in Jerusalem – what he taught about it, and the safeguards he put into place around it – are revealing and instructive for us. They show Paul's strong sense of accountability, transparency, and integrity. His example and his teaching apply just as much now to the financial affairs of churches and missions as they did in his day.

Paul makes use of the collection as an occasion for significant teaching. In fact, he gives more textual space in his letters to writing about this financial matter than he does to writing about justification by faith. That probably surprises us. Saying this, of course, is not in any sense to belittle Paul's doctrine of justification or any of his great doctrinal teaching. But it does remind us that he considered Christian giving to be a matter of great theological importance also.

We will look at three major passages and a few shorter ones so as to draw some principles from these texts. The major passages are 1 Corinthians 16, where he refers to this collection; 2 Corinthians 8–9, where he devotes a great deal of space to principles of giving; and then Romans 15. In these passages, we see at least six clear principles at work.

1. Financial Support for the Poor Is Integral to Biblical Mission

Paul sees no dichotomy between his evangelistic church planting mission and his efforts to bring about the relief of poverty among the believers in Jerusalem. For Paul this is all part of his task, his mission, and his calling.

Galatians 2

Before turning to those major texts, let's step sideways for a moment to Galatians 2. In Galatians, Paul is defending three things: (1) his own apostolic authority; (2) the content of his apostolic gospel; and (3) the rightness of his preaching of the gospel to the Gentiles. The *Galati* were a branch of the great nations of the Celts who had migrated into what we now call southern Turkey. Paul had preached the gospel to them, and they had become believers in Jesus Christ. Then Paul faced some bitter theological controversy with the Jewish believers as to how these non-Jewish people could be accepted into the covenant and into the people of God. Some of the Jewish believers had come to Galatia and troubled the Galatian churches, trying to insist that they must become circumcised and observe the Mosaic law.

Paul writes the Epistle to the Galatians against that background in order to defend the fact that his gospel had been accepted as fully authentic by the apostles in Jerusalem itself. That is what chapter 2 is all about. He states that he had received his teaching from the Lord but had submitted it to the apostles in Jerusalem, and they had accepted that it was authentic and true.

So Paul affirms:

> James, Cephas [i.e. Peter] and John, those esteemed as pillars, gave me and Barnabas the right hand of fellowship [*koinonia*] when they recognized the grace given to me. They agreed that we should go to the Gentiles, and they to the circumcised. All they asked was that we should continue to remember the poor, the very thing I had been eager to do all along. (Gal 2:9–10)

The "right hand of fellowship" in verse 9 is not simply a token of friendship. The Greek word *koinonia* means much more. It is a sharing *in*, and a sharing *of*, what God has given to us, and that affects the economic dimension as well as the spiritual dimension. So in Acts 2 and 4, we read about the *koinonia* of the early church in Jerusalem. Certainly, it was a spiritual *koinonia*. Believers shared in the apostles' teaching, in the breaking of bread, and in prayers. But it was also a financial *koinonia* in which they shared with one another in order to relieve poverty.

It is clear from what Paul says in Galatians 2 that that spirit of the church in Jerusalem was still operating; the Jerusalem church still cared about the poor in their midst. They saw it as an essential part of gospel *koinonia* that if Paul the apostle was going to be a partner with them and share in their understanding of the gospel, then he too must be committed to remembering the poor as part of his gospel credentials. And Paul says, "That was no problem to me. I was eagerly doing that already." We can see that active financial concern for the poor is how the Jerusalem church operated, and it was also part of Paul's missional commitment.

Romans 15

Let's turn now to Romans 15. Here at the very end of his letter, Paul is telling the Roman church about his plans. He writes about his lifelong commitment to church planting and evangelistic ministry. Earlier in the chapter, he explained how God had given him grace "to be a minister of Jesus Christ to the Gentiles . . . [with] the priestly duty of proclaiming the gospel of God, so that the Gentiles might become an offering acceptable to God" (vv. 15–16). That has been his life's ministry, and it is still what Paul believes God has called him to continue. But he has now done it all around the *eastern* Mediterranean basin, all the way from Jerusalem to Illyricum, now modern Albania. Paul says,

> I have fully proclaimed the gospel of Christ. It has always been my ambition to preach the gospel where Christ was not known, so that I would not be building on someone else's foundation. . . . But now . . . there is no more place for me to work in these regions. (Rom 15:19–20, 23)

So now Paul is planning a bold missionary project that will take him to the *western* half of the Mediterranean, out toward Spain (v. 24). That is his great evangelistic vision. But *at the moment*, says Paul, his priority is that he is on the way to Jerusalem in the service of the saints there. That is what he must do next.

> For Macedonia and Achaia were pleased to make a contribution for the poor among the Lord's people in Jerusalem. They were pleased to do it, and indeed they owe it to them. For if the Gentiles have shared in the Jews' spiritual blessings, they owe it to the Jews to share with them their material blessings. So after I have completed this task and have made sure that they have received this contribution, I will go to Spain and visit you on the way. I know that when I come to you, I will come in the full measure of the blessing of Christ. (Rom 15:26–29)

Look carefully at what he says a bit later, verses 31–32: "Pray that I may be kept safe from the unbelievers in Judea and that the contribution I take to Jerusalem may be favorably received by the Lord's people there, so that I may come to you with joy, by God's will, and in your company be refreshed."

Paul in effect puts his *evangelistic strategy* on hold in order to carry out his *relief of poverty strategy*. It is interesting that at this point Paul does not say, "I've got to go on to evangelize Spain, so I'll dump the responsibility for this financial gift onto somebody else; *they* can take it to Jerusalem. *My* job is to preach the gospel, not to relieve the poor." Paul sees no conflict at all in making a priority at this point in his life of his service to the saints through the relief of poverty by taking collected money to the people in Jerusalem.

Not only does Paul see it as a personal priority; he asks for prayer for it. He asks for prayer just as later he would ask for prayer when he was in prison, when he asked people to pray for him to have courage to preach the gospel. Just as he called on believers to pray for him in his *evangelistic* ministry, here he asks the Roman Christians to pray for him in his *financial* ministry to the saints in Jerusalem.

Paul did not perceive this task as some unfortunate interruption in his evangelistic career which he sadly cannot avoid. Rather, by completing this work of poverty relief, he will be fulfilling a joyfully *Christ-centred* calling, just as much as when he was completing his evangelistic mandate.

So it is clear that Paul sees no dichotomy between these two dimensions of his ministry. Indeed, as one writer has said, "We do not know if Paul achieved this mission [his evangelistic plans to go to Spain], but we do know that he delivered the collection [to relieve the poor in Jerusalem]. *The collection was so vital that its delivery was at that moment a more urgent matter for Paul than his desire to evangelize and plant churches on the missionary frontier.*"[1]

In 1 Timothy 6, Paul instructs Timothy to pass this teaching on to the church. The responsibility for generous giving by those who have the means to do so is a fundamental part of Christian commitment and a part of our response to the gospel and our investment in God's future. Paul says:

> Command those who are rich in this present world not to be arrogant nor to put their hope in wealth, which is so uncertain, but to put their hope in God, who richly provides us with everything for our enjoyment. Command them [repeated for emphasis] to do good, to be rich in good deeds, and to be generous and willing to share. In this way they will lay up treasure for

---

1. Jason Hood, "Theology in Action: Paul and Christian Social Care," in *Transforming the World: The Gospel and Social Responsibility*, eds. Jamie A. Grant and Dewi A. Hughes, 129–146 (Nottingham: Apollos, 2009). Quotation from 134; emphasis original.

themselves as a firm foundation for the coming age, so that they may take hold of the life that is truly life. (1 Tim 6:17–19)

The English "willing to share" conceals the fact that the Greek word is *koinonikos* (fellowship). They are to prove their fellowship by their financial generosity, and in this way, they will lay up treasure for themselves as a firm foundation for the coming age, echoing the teaching of Jesus.

Generosity is a Christian duty, says Paul, something that pastors can command. He is probably echoing Deuteronomy 15, where God says to the Israelites,

> Give generously to them [the poor] and do so without a grudging heart; then because of this the LORD your God will bless you in all your work and in everything you put your hand to. There will always be poor people in the land. Therefore I command you to be openhanded toward your fellow Israelites who are poor and needy in your land. . . .
>
> Supply them liberally from your flock, your threshing floor and your winepress. Give to them as the LORD your God has blessed you. Remember that you were slaves in Egypt and the LORD your God redeemed you. That is why I give you this command today. (Deut 15:10–11, 14–15)

Summary Principle 1: *Paul saw generous financial support for the poor and careful administration of that gift as an integral part of biblical mission, of gospel mission. It was part of what he believed that he himself was called to do as an apostle, as well as the more obviously evangelistic task of church planting and discipling.*

2. Financial Administration Is a Stewardship of Grace and Obedience

When we handle money that has been given by God's people, we are handling (1) the fruit of God's grace and (2) the practical proof of human obedience to the gospel. That is the implication of these two chapters. Money that has been given as an offering to God is not just "stuff." It is not just coins and notes or ledgers or pieces of paper or entries in a journal. When we handle money that has been given by God's people, we are involved in a deeply spiritual matter. Their giving is their response to God, and our involvement is a stewardship of God's grace and a stewardship of other people's obedience. That is what stewardship means: we are entrusted with something; we are stewards of something that is the fruit of grace and the proof of obedience.

Grace

On this point, of course, we are echoing John Stott's first principle in part two. Three times in 2 Corinthians 8:1–7, Paul uses the word "grace" about the Macedonian believers, and a couple verses later he talks about "the *grace* of our Lord Jesus Christ" (v. 9).

This gift of the Macedonians, Paul writes, was a response to the Lord: "They gave themselves first of all to the Lord" (v. 5). Moreover, it was something that they wanted to do. They did not have to be asked to give; rather, they asked for the privilege of giving. Further, Paul says it was because of that grace of God in them that what they did was an act of grace to others. This is reciprocal grace, or grace in action. Grace received and grace passed on.

Paul then sends Titus to oversee and administer the collection. It is as if Paul were to say (and I think this is the flavour of his wording), "Because this is such an important evidence of the grace of God and of the fruit of the gospel in the lives of these new Gentile believers, I am sending my most trusted senior person to handle this responsibility." Paul did not send some young functionary who might be haphazard in dealing with it all. Paul says in effect, "This is a serious matter, so we urged Titus – an important apostolic delegate in the church – to go and make sure that this *act of grace* will be properly handled and treated with the due diligence that it deserves."

Obedience

This display of generosity was not just an act of grace, but also an act of obedience.

> This service that you perform is not only supplying the needs of the Lord's people but is also overflowing in many expressions of thanks to God. Because of the service by which you have proved yourselves, others will praise God for the obedience that accompanies your confession of the gospel of Christ, and for your generosity in sharing with them and with everyone else. And in their prayers for you their hearts will go out to you, because of the surpassing grace God has given you. Thanks be to God for his indescribable gift! (2 Cor 9:12–15)

And of course, Paul means God's "indescribable gift" of his Son, Jesus Christ.

According to Paul, giving, sharing, and generosity are not just grace; they are also proof of obedience. Why was that important? Precisely because these were Gentiles. The Jewish believers in Jerusalem were still uncertain whether or not these Gentiles, who had never been circumcised and were not observing all the law, were really part of God's family. Did they really belong to the covenant people of God? Paul responds in effect, "The fact that you Gentiles have given an offering to meet the needs of Jewish believers is a proof of the fellowship that we have in Christ. Your obedience to the gospel is a demonstration that you Gentiles, who have been so despised by the Jews historically, are now one with them in the Messiah Jesus. There is no difference, there is no Jew or Gentile, male or female, slave or free." Let's not miss the profound theological significance here. Paul is talking gospel truth and showing how it could be modelled and authenticated. This gift was a proof of obedience to the core meaning and reconciling power of the gospel.

Summary Principle 2: Handling a gift offered by God's people is a sacred trust. Administering it is a stewardship of the grace of God and of the obedience of God's people to the gospel. Paul takes it very seriously and so should we. Paul's demand for accountability, integrity, and transparency was not just to satisfy the Roman governors or other officials. It was because he was dealing with something coming from God: the grace of God and obedience to the gospel.

3. Financial Appeals Require Systematic Advance Planning

Look how thoroughly Paul prepares the way for the gift. In 1 Corinthians, he has been answering a lot of questions from the church, and in chapter 16, he comes back to something that he has told them about before, but wants to raise again. So he says:

> Now about the collection for the Lord's people:
> Do what I told the Galatian churches to do. On
> the first day of every week, each one of you should

> set aside a sum of money in keeping with your
> income, saving it up, so that when I come no
> collections will have to be made. Then, when I
> arrive, I will give letters of introduction to the
> men you approve and send them with your gift
> to Jerusalem. (1 Cor 16:1–3)

Get ready for this, says Paul. Make your preparations well in advance.

In his second letter, Paul shows the same concern for preparedness.

> There is no need for me to write to you about
> this service to the Lord's people. For I know
> your eagerness to help, and I have been boasting
> about it to the Macedonians, telling them that
> since last year you in Achaia were ready to give;
> and your enthusiasm has stirred most of them
> to action. But I am sending the brothers in order
> that our boasting about you in this matter should
> not prove hollow, but that you may be ready, as I
> said you would be. For if any Macedonians come
> with me and find you unprepared, we – not to say
> anything about you – would be ashamed of having
> been so confident. So I thought it necessary to
> urge the brothers to visit you in advance and
> finish the arrangements for the generous gift you
> had promised. Then it will be ready as a generous
> gift, not as one grudgingly given. (2 Cor 9:1–5)

Can you see what Paul is doing here? He does not want this collection to become debased into an emotional appeal in which everybody is urged to put their hands in their pockets, and the music goes on and on until everybody has dug deeper, and then the offering buckets are sent around again. No, Paul is purposely avoiding that type of manipulated, emotional response in giving. He does not want there to be any kind of "on-the-spot" pressure or a response that has not been carefully thought through in advance. Paul wants his collection and the giving by the church to be something that has been thought about, prayed about, and prepared for.

Christian giving should be systematic: you plan what you will give. It should be regular: week by week setting money aside. It should be proportionate: according to income, with those who have more giving more. It should be transparent: several people will oversee it. And it should be public: announced and recorded. All of this preparation and supervision is built into the arrangements that Paul is carefully planning in advance. He put a lot of thought into this.

So we need to learn that accountability is not just an afterthought. It is not something you try to sort out *after the event*, when you realize, "All this money has come in; how wonderful! Now we'd better decide what we do with it, who is going to count it, who is going to bank it, and who will keep accounts." No, that should all be planned beforehand.

Accountability is not just a matter of reacting when problems or questions arise. It should be planned; it should be built in from the very start. Paul says in effect, "Look, here is the plan. This is what we're asking *you* to do, and this is what *we* will then do when you have done what we ask." The whole procedure is a matter of shared responsibility. Paul did not want their giving to be mere opportunism. He did not want them to be saying to one another after he had arrived, "Hey! Paul has come to town again! Let's have a quick collection and give him a love gift." No, Paul wants this offering (for others, not for himself) to be carefully thought through and planned well in advance, so that nobody will be taken by surprise, and nobody can be accused of emotional manipulation. That is an important way in which he builds accountability into his financial relationship with the church.

Notice that Paul is concerned, also, about loss of face. The world of ancient Greece and Rome was a very relational economy, based on relationships of honour, obligations, and potential shame. So Paul conducts this offering relationally. He says in effect, "Some of our brothers will be coming to you, and I will be coming later as well, and we don't want any embarrassment. I don't want you to lose face. I don't want you to be ashamed, and I don't want others to be gloating. So let's do this properly. Let's plan it well ahead and have it all out on the table clear and open, so that everybody is satisfied."

Summary Principle 3: Proper planning in advance of financial appeals is important, and safeguards should be set up around financial giving before *the event, not just tacked on afterwards.*

4. Financial Temptations Call for "Safety in Numbers"

Wherever there is money, there is temptation. This is just as true for Christians as anybody else, so it is wise to protect ourselves from such temptation by having more than one person involved in handling the money. This way of working was true of Paul's ministry in general. Of course, Paul was a great individual minister, preacher, letter writer, and everything else. But generally he did not operate alone. He was the leader, but he worked with teams that included people like Silas, Barnabas, Timothy, Titus, and so on. Indeed, when Paul did find himself completely alone, he was very distressed about it. In 2 Timothy 4:16, there are some heart-rending words when he says that everyone had deserted him; this was terrible for him. He wanted to be in a team; he wanted to belong with others.

That is why, then, in 1 Corinthians 16 and 2 Corinthians 8, Paul lays great emphasis on the plurality of people involved in handling the money. Knowing exactly who was involved becomes quite complicated for us to figure out, but there were plenty of them.

Look first at 1 Corinthians 16:3–4. Paul says, "I will give letters of introduction to the men you approve and send them with your gift to Jerusalem" – in other words, people whom the Christians in Corinth trusted. Paul then offers to share the task himself. He adds, "If it seems advisable for me to go also, they will accompany me." So Paul would not take charge of the money by himself but would involve others in that major responsibility.

It is also difficult to know how many people are involved in 2 Corinthians 8:16–24, but we can identify some.

> Thanks be to God, who put into the heart of Titus the same concern I have for you. For Titus not only welcomed our appeal, but he is coming to you with much enthusiasm and on his own initiative. And we are sending along with him the brother who is praised by all the churches for his service to the gospel. What is more, he was chosen by the churches to accompany us as we carry the offering. (2 Cor 8:16–19)

We don't know this other person's name, but he was a trusted Christian leader along with Titus.

A little later Paul adds,

> In addition, we are sending with them our brother who has often proved to us in many ways that he is zealous, and now even more so because of his great confidence in you. (2 Cor 8:22)

Again, we don't know who this is, but Paul deemed him trustworthy.

So as I say, we can't be sure exactly how many people Paul had in mind. But the point is that certainly more than one person was involved, at least three in addition to Paul himself. And they were all trusted people. They were accepted and known by everybody. There was no secrecy.

Christian accountability is a matter of trust, and we may well believe and expect that we should be able to trust our fellow believers. Yes indeed, but Paul shows us the wisdom of building in safeguards of plurality, because even believers are still sinners and few things are more tempting than money. Paul is well aware that even trusted brothers and sisters can go astray. Sadly, we read about a few of them at the end of some of his letters, when he writes that some of his former companions who preferred the world and the world's ways have gone off and left him (e.g. 2 Tim 4:10). Paul knew that even the best people need the protection of relational accountability to one another.

So then, Paul insists on plurality in the handling of money. It is a very wise principle to adopt in any church or Christian organization. In many UK churches, certainly in my own church at All Souls, Langham Place, gift money is never counted by only one person. When the offering is brought to the vestry, there are always at least two and sometimes three or four people in the room. The door is then closed, and they count the offering together. They are a check on one another. Now of course, we all trust one another; nobody expects that anybody is going to be doing anything wrong. But there is need for openness and verifiability in handling money. We need to be above suspicion.

Many Christian organizations, including my own (Langham Partnership), will not allow large bank cheques to be signed by only one person; there must always be two signatures to manage the bank account and the finances. That is another wise practice.

How do we make this work in some countries and cultures where it is quite unthinkable to question the honour and the authority of senior leaders – least of all by calling them to account over money? I know that in some Asian cultures, it is simply not appropriate, and never done, for anybody to challenge or question leaders, especially if they are older. That would be to break the relationship and cause loss of face. Christians in senior leadership seem to be routinely regarded as above questioning by anybody "beneath" them. So what can be done to ensure proper accountability?

It seems to me that the only way is for the *leaders themselves* (and it usually seems to be a man, but of course the same would apply to a woman) to *choose voluntarily* to say, "Please, will you join me in this? I request and insist that other people should be involved with me as we arrange our financial affairs, or as we handle these funds, or as we set up this institution. I want other people alongside myself to see how the money is handled and accounted for, and how all decisions are made about how it is spent. I want the rest of the congregation, or staff, or donors to be completely satisfied that all is being done transparently and honourably. And I am using my authority in the church or organization to set this in place and submit myself to it." That is, he *exercises* his authority by choosing to *submit* his authority to the scrutiny of others in this matter. That is fully biblical.

In that way, the person "at the top" is able to lead from the top and to set the example of transparency and accountability. And this would be to imitate the apostle Paul himself. Think about how senior he was, and what authority he had as an apostle of Christ. Paul could easily have said, "Trust me. I'm an apostle. I'll take charge of this money myself." But he did not. He insisted *from the top* that there should be others alongside him to ensure it was all done honestly.

If leaders do this *voluntarily*, they are not saying to those under them, "I think you don't trust me." Rather they are saying, "I know that you do trust me. And because you trust me, I want to make sure that your trust is never betrayed. I want to avoid all temptation. I want to be completely transparent, and therefore I *choose* to share my accountability with other trusted Christian brothers and sisters."

Summary Principle 4: *In order to introduce higher standards of accountability, we must lead by example from above, rather than be faced with demands or suspicion from below. Accountability is something we as leaders should choose to have, for our own good and for the protection of the Lord's name, not as something that is forced upon us.*

5. Financial Accountability Demands Transparency before God and Human Beings

I love the fact that when Paul has finished talking about all the people he is bringing into the team to deliver the money to Jerusalem, he actually explains why he is handling it in this plural way. Paul says:

> We want to avoid any criticism of the way we administer this liberal gift. *For we are taking pains to do what is right, not only in the eyes of the Lord but also in the eyes of man.* (2 Cor 8:20–21; my emphasis)

These verses express a principle that is transcultural. That is, it provides a biblical model for us, whatever our culture or background. They are challenging and very significant. I think they should be hung up on the wall of any room where a Christian organization does its financial business.

All the arrangements that Paul put in place were not only very careful, they were also probably quite costly. It would obviously cost a lot more for four or five men to travel from

Greece to Jerusalem than for Paul to go there by himself; travel was not cheap in those days any more than today.

So the arrangements Paul was building up around this gift could have aroused resistance. People could have criticized and said, "Why send so many people? You are going to waste some of the gift on such expenses" (just as we complain about the cost of auditing our accounts). But Paul says in effect, "It's worth that cost because I don't want to be vulnerable to any accusation of fraud or misappropriation of this precious gift; I want to be completely transparent before God and people, so that nothing we do can be open to criticism later."

Paul was operating within a culture which in certain respects was quite similar to some non-Western cultures today. The Greek and Roman cultures were very top-down, very hierarchical. The Roman system was patron-client oriented. The men at the top were patrons: they were bankers or politicians, they were wealthy, and people would come to their homes every day wanting favours. Being in with the powerful man or the wealthy man was crucially important; that is how Roman politics worked.

So Paul is acting counterculturally in what he does with this gift. He could have said, "I'm the boss; I'm your patron; I'm the apostle. Give me the money and pay for a single armed guard, and I'll take it to Jerusalem. Just trust me." Instead he says in effect, "No, I want this to be completely transparent, so I must have others with me to make sure all is done properly and above criticism."

I would love 2 Corinthians 8:21 to become a motto for each of us as Christ's followers, to be something that we could take to heart: "We are taking pains to do what is right, not only in the eyes of the Lord [we all want to do that] but also in the eyes of man." What a difference it could make if all Christian organizations were totally committed to Paul's fundamental principle here, and how it could help to prevent some of the tragic scandals of fraud and theft and mismanagement within Christian organizations.

Summary Principle 5: Vertical and the horizontal accountability are both needed. Paul means, "We should be able to trust one another in the Lord, but we want to do what is beyond criticism in the eyes of the watching world as well."

6. Financial Trustworthiness Is an Apostolic Honour to Christ

Think for a moment about upward and downward accountability. We tend to think that we are *upwardly* accountable to other bodies such as boards and funding foundations and donors and the government and legal authorities, and that we are *downwardly* accountable to our beneficiaries, that is, to those who actually receive from our ministry, those whom we are serving. Actually, however, the direction of our accountability is the reverse. Our *upward* accountability is to those who occupy the position Jesus was referring to when he said, "Truly I tell you, whatever you did for one of the least of these brothers and sisters of mine, you did for me" (Matt 25:40). It is those whom our ministry is serving who actually are Jesus to us. Therefore our accountability to *them* is really our accountability to *him* – which is "upward." When we serve others in our ministry, we are serving Christ. We are honouring him in serving them. That is our primary accountability.

Paul says in several passages that discharging financial responsibility in a trustworthy manner is an honour to Christ, not just a matter of transparency before people. Of course it is important to do the job with honesty and integrity. But even more, it is important to do it for the honour and glory of Christ.

Look first at 2 Corinthians 8:18–19. Who were these people who were administering the gift? Paul says, "We are sending along with him [Titus] the brother who is praised by all the churches for his service to the gospel. What is more, he was chosen by the churches." This other man, then, was an honoured person whose life was already seen to be honouring to the Lord and honouring to the gospel. For that reason, Paul and the Corinthians could trust him with their money. And the way he handles the money will also be honouring to the Lord and to the church. Honest finances are honouring to Christ (with the obvious implication that dishonesty dishonours Christ).

Paul then makes the point even more explicitly.

> As for Titus, he is my partner and co-worker among you; as for our brothers, they are representatives of the churches and *an honour to Christ.* Therefore show these men the proof of your love and the reason for our pride in you, so that the churches can see it. (2 Cor 8:23–24; my emphasis)

The Greek word used there and translated "representatives" is actually *apostoloi*, apostles. It is used in the weaker sense that occurs several times in the New Testament to refer to others beyond the twelve apostolic pillars of the church: the twelve disciples, minus Judas Iscariot and plus Matthias in the Book of Acts, and then the apostle Paul. In this slightly looser sense, the word *apostolos* meant someone who was an emissary or a trusted delegate of the churches. There seem to have been a number of these apostolic delegates going around the churches – Titus, Timothy, Andronicus and Junia (Rom 16:7), and others who are mentioned in 3 John and elsewhere. So Paul says these *apostoloi*, these chosen delegates of the churches who are being entrusted with the responsibility of handling finances within the churches, especially this large financial gift to Jerusalem, are "an honour to Christ" (2 Cor 8:23).

What a commendation! What a way to speak of an accountant or a treasurer! These persons are entrusted with money. And by being faithful in that trust, they are not only an honour to Christ, but also they should have church approval: "show these men the proof of your love and the reason for our pride in you, so that the churches can see it" (v. 24).

Another example is Epaphroditus. Look at how Paul speaks about him in Philippians 2:25–30. He says,

> I think it is necessary to send back to you Epaphroditus, my brother, co-worker and fellow soldier, who is also your messenger . . . (Phil 2:25)

The Greek word translated "messenger" here is *apostolos* again. Now, Epaphroditus was not an apostle in the sense that Paul was, but he was the emissary, the representative, the trusted messenger of the church, and hence "apostolic." Paul continues,

> . . . whom you sent to take care of my needs. For he longs for all of you and is distressed because you heard he was ill. Indeed he was ill, and almost died. But God had mercy on him, and not on him only but also on me, to spare me sorrow upon sorrow. Therefore I am all the more eager to send him, so that when you see him again you may be glad and I may have less anxiety. So then, welcome him in the Lord with great joy, and honour people like him, because he almost died for the work of Christ. He risked his life to make up for the help you yourselves could not give me. (Phil 2:25–30)

What Paul is describing is Epaphroditus's handling of the financial and material gift that the Philippian church had made to Paul when he was in need. And Paul says essentially, "That service of Epaphroditus was a work of the gospel; that was a work born out of love for Christ and for his church." Epaphroditus nearly died doing what he did for his church and for Paul, so therefore Paul says, "Honour him. He does what he does for Christ's sake."

Later on, in Philippians 4:14–19, we find another reference to the same thing: the gift that the Philippian believers had sent to Paul through Epaphroditus. Paul comments,

> I have received full payment and have more than enough. I am amply supplied, now that I have received from Epaphroditus the gifts you sent. They are a fragrant offering, an acceptable sacrifice, pleasing to God. (Phil 4:18)

Epaphroditus's role then, says Paul, was an apostolic honour: serving God and serving Christ by serving the servants of God. In serving the servants of God, people like Epaphroditus who handle the church's gifts are deserving of honour and respect because they are an honour to Christ himself.

To administer financial affairs with trustworthiness, with honesty, and diligence, like Epaphroditus and others in the New Testament, is a Christ-honouring thing to do: we do it for him.

When I was the principal of All Nations Christian College near London, there was a time when issues arose that affected me personally. At that time the chairman of the college board of directors was a very wise, godly brother whom I greatly respected. I was required to give account of some aspects of how I was running things and decisions that had been made. That was not easy; it is not comfortable to have people poking into everything that is going on. That is true even if you have nothing troubling your conscience. I knew that in relation to the college, I had done nothing wrong, but still I had to accept the questioning, even though I did not like it.

At one point, the chairman of the council came privately to my office and said to me, "Chris, accountability is not a burden; it's a *gift*. It's a gift that we as the board give to you as our principal. We hold you accountable, and that is for *your* good; it's for your protection. It's not something we are imposing upon you. It's something we are *giving* to you because we love you, because you are a brother in Christ, and we want to affirm your integrity by expecting proper accountability."

I thought that was a very helpful, positive way for me to look at the demanding challenge of accountability. I learned to see accountability not as a threat or an insult or "beneath my dignity to be questioned," but rather as something that was honouring to me and also, of course, to God.

Summary Principle 6: *God himself says, "Those who honour me I will honour (1 Sam 2:30). If we want the Lord's honour, then we need to be honourable in the way in which we handle our finances and in the way we are accountable; we need to be men and women of integrity in all that we seek to do for him. Let us make Paul and his teaching on this matter a powerful and authoritative model for ourselves.*

May we all pray for God to grant us the courage to live and work with complete integrity, and may we honour one another by expecting – and giving – accountability to one another and to the Lord.

Epilogue

The Personal Journey of a "Kingdom Builder"

James Cousins

Making a Decision to Follow Jesus

It all started when youth workers from a local church presented the gospel to me. I trusted the Lord Jesus Christ as my Saviour on August 20, 1964 (age thirteen).

I spent forty years (age fifteen to fifty-five) in the "wilderness of business" just making money. I started by saying that I was going to keep God first in our business, but like most others, the business controlled me, and God had to take second place. During those forty years, I looked like a respectable Christian business man going to church each week with my family and giving some of my hard-earned money to the Lord's work. But deep within me, I knew I had lost focus so many times through my disobedience of God's word. Although I had let my Lord and Saviour down, he never let me down.

When I was fifty-five, my wife and I both came to the realization that all we possessed belonged to our Lord and Saviour and that it had been given to us for the extension of his kingdom. We also realized that we had only been playing about at giving to the Lord's work, and our prayer for the future was that over the next fifteen years, God willing, we wanted to do all we could to help ministries to bring Jesus to the nations through "ministry support."

In hindsight, during those forty years in the "wilderness of business" I had been living in a two-kingdom world. You see, there was God's part of my life where God was King, and the rest which was my business world and I was king. The Lord was saying to me, "If you want to serve me, there can only be one King, and if I am not King of all, then I am not King at all."

When my wife and I realized that there can be only one King in our lives, we decided to go from giving the Lord the minority of what he had blessed us with to giving the Lord the majority of what he had blessed us with.

That was when we started our new "journey of generosity."

Why Me, Lord?

The question "Why me, Lord?" had always been a big question in my life. At the age of twenty-one, I was involved in a boating accident with two friends, the end result being that they were both lost at sea. This event took me into a very dark period in my life with the question always in my mind, "Why me, Lord?" Why had God taken my two friends and not me? I never had any time for school; I just wanted to get a manual job and start working as soon as possible. I believe that Jesus has a way of turning things upside down, because in my business I developed skills in the financial administration sector which allowed the business to prosper. So again, at the end of each year when the profits were going up and up, I kept asking the same old question, "Why me, Lord?" I could not understand how a guy with such a poor education could make so much money!

What Had the Lord Planned for My Life?

At age fifty-five when I started to reflect on my past years and to think about the next fifteen years, if God would grant them, it became very clear that the gifts we had been given by the Lord were all in the area of "ministry support," so we started to study and think about what that means. Often, it seemed that perceptions and realities in this area did not match up.

Many times people, including Chris Wright earlier in this book, have quoted the famous words of Hudson Taylor, "God's work, done in God's way, will never lack God's supply." But what I could not understand was why so many good ministries that I believed were doing "God's work" were without question lacking "God's supply." What was wrong? I did not think for one second that God was at fault; there had to be something we were doing wrong within the middle part of the quote "done in God's way." So I turned to study the Bible to find the answer.

So many people did not want to discuss the subject of "ministry support." They just quoted, "But when you give to the needy, do not let your left hand know what your right hand is doing" (Matt 6:3). They said that I was talking about "fundraising" and that the Bible does not agree with "fundraising." But in my own study of the Scriptures, I found the *opposite* to be true. The Lord used people like Moses, David, and Paul to talk to the people about "fundraising." If you take the time to study these three stories, you will be surprised at the outcome. When Moses asked the people for help, he got so much that he had to *stop* the people giving. David led the people by the example of his own giving, then all his friends followed him, and together they met the "ministry need." When Paul approached the Macedonian people, he says, "they urgently pleaded with us for the privilege of sharing in this service to the Lord's people" (2 Cor 8:4).

I was amazed at the number of times that after a wonderful ministry presentation by people who were doing their best to make Jesus known among the nations, they ended up by saying, "But we have a small problem; we need a little extra support." This statement I believed was wrong. You see, the problem did *not* belong to the "ministry people," but it did belong to the "ministry *support* people" – people whom God had blessed with the resources to meet the ministry need.

Who Are Kingdom Builders, and What Do We Believe?

As we emphasised in part 1, all disciples of Jesus Christ are called to be kingdom builders, serving him in every walk of life and giving generously to support God's work in multiple ways. Some of us as well to whom God has entrusted more than average income and wealth are called to be among what we might call 1 percent kingdom builders. Emphatically we claim no greater *righteousness* than any other believer, but just as emphatically and biblically, we do shoulder a greater *responsibility* because of the greater capacity that God has given us.

Over the last few years, a number of business and professional people have been working together to try and go "from addition to multiplication" of both ministry and ministry support. We are just a group of God's people who are very interested in the advancement of God's kingdom. So we have been calling ourselves, "kingdom builders." We acknowledge with humility and gratitude that we are among that 1 percent.

In Acts 18:9–10 (ESV) we read, "And the Lord said to Paul one night in a vision, 'Do not be afraid . . . for I am with you . . . for I have many in this city who are my people.'" We believe that God has his people in every city of the world. Most of God's people who have a heart to support kingdom ministries want to remain anonymous, so we have chosen the name "kingdom builders" when we talk between one another. We have begun to experience business and professional people working together in partnership by using the gifts that the Lord has given them for the extension of his kingdom.

We have some core values. Kingdom builders are trying to prioritize what is important in life. We believe that it is more blessed to give than to receive, so we are now starting on a new "journey of generosity." This journey starts with "nominal generosity" but has a goal of reaching "*radical generosity*" – radical generosity in all three main areas of our lives: time, talents, and treasures.

Kingdom builders believe in "*integrity, transparency, accountability*, and *humility*." We encourage ministries always to be transparent and accountable when working with kingdom builders. We also love the verse that Chris Wright has highlighted in part 3, "for we aim at what is honourable not only in the Lord's sight but also in the sight of man" (2 Cor 8:21, ESV). We take that verse as a kind of motto. Accountability is so important in ministry in two ways. Any ministry should be held totally accountable at all times to its ministry partners. But on the other hand, kingdom builders should be held totally accountable for the "ministry shortfall." God has blessed them "for such a time as this."

Is God Calling You to Be a Kingdom Builder?

- Have you trusted the Lord Jesus Christ as your own personal Saviour?
- Do you work in the business or professional world?
- Do you believe that your ability to make money is a gift from God?
- Do you believe that the money you make now belongs to God?

If you have answered yes to the above questions, did you know that you have become an investment manager in the biggest bank in the world? It belongs to the "King of Kings and Lord of Lords." He is calling you to invest *his* money wisely in his kingdom. Remember that all the gifts that we possess were given to us by God.

- *The salvation gift!* "For by grace you have been saved through faith. And this is not your own doing; it is the gift of God, not a result of works, so that no one may boast" (Eph 2:8–9, ESV).
- *The good works gift!* "For we are his workmanship, created in Christ Jesus for good works, which God prepared beforehand, that we should walk in them" (Eph 2:10, ESV).

Throughout our lives, we have been blessed by the greatest gift of all; God gave his Son to die for us. Now he wants us to give to others so that the story of Jesus can go to all the people of the world. In light of his great radical and sacrificial generosity to us, we have a clear answer to the problem of the shortfall.

The problem of the shortfall is the responsibility of kingdom builders – all of them, whether in the 99 percent or the 1 percent. We will be held accountable. And for those of us who are blessed to be in the 1 percent, God has a unique work for us to do as kingdom builders!

Conclusion

When I look back over the past fourteen years of my study of ministry support and think about "perception or reality" in relation to what is the most important thing in my life, I remember that I have spent most of my life "doing" and "fixing" things. And of course, all through this essay of my personal journey as a kingdom builder, I have been encouraging *you* to "do" things!

However as we try to prioritize what is most important in our lives, I now believe with all my heart that what the Lord is saying to me is, "Stop doing and start being." God wants me to seek intimacy with himself through prayer and his word. Ultimately, this is not just a matter of building better relationships between ministry people and ministry support people, but for all of us to be cultivating a deeper relationship with the Lord himself.

That is where it all starts – and ends.

Langham Literature and its imprints are a ministry of Langham Partnership.

Langham Partnership is a global fellowship working in pursuit of the vision God entrusted to its founder John Stott –

> *to facilitate the growth of the church in maturity and Christ-likeness through raising the standards of biblical preaching and teaching.*

Our vision is to see churches in the Majority World equipped for mission and growing to maturity in Christ through the ministry of pastors and leaders who believe, teach and live by the word of God.

Our mission is to strengthen the ministry of the word of God through:
- nurturing national movements for biblical preaching
- fostering the creation and distribution of evangelical literature
- enhancing evangelical theological education

especially in countries where churches are under-resourced.

Our ministry

Langham Preaching partners with national leaders to nurture indigenous biblical preaching movements for pastors and lay preachers all around the world. With the support of a team of trainers from many countries, a multi-level programme of seminars provides practical training, and is followed by a programme for training local facilitators. Local preachers' groups and national and regional networks ensure continuity and ongoing development, seeking to build vigorous movements committed to Bible exposition.

Langham Literature provides Majority World preachers, scholars and seminary libraries with evangelical books and electronic resources through publishing and distribution, grants and discounts. The programme also fosters the creation of indigenous evangelical books in many languages, through writer's grants, strengthening local evangelical publishing houses, and investment in major regional literature projects, such as one volume Bible commentaries like *The Africa Bible Commentary* and *The South Asia Bible Commentary*.

Langham Scholars provides financial support for evangelical doctoral students from the Majority World so that, when they return home, they may train pastors and other Christian leaders with sound, biblical and theological teaching. This programme equips those who equip others. Langham Scholars also works in partnership with Majority World seminaries in strengthening evangelical theological education. A growing number of Langham Scholars study in high quality doctoral programmes in the Majority World itself. As well as teaching the next generation of pastors, graduated Langham Scholars exercise significant influence through their writing and leadership.

To learn more about Langham Partnership and the work we do visit **langham.org**